MW00781776

# Unarmed and Dangerous

There is tremendous controversy across the United States (and beyond) when a police officer uses deadly force against an unarmed citizen, but often the conversation is devoid of contextual details. These details matter greatly as a matter of law and organizational legitimacy. In this short book, authors Jon Shane and Zoë Swenson offer a comprehensive analysis of the first study to use publicly available data to reveal some of the context in which an officer used deadly force against an unarmed citizen. Although any police shooting, even a justified shooting, is not a desired outcome—often termed "lawful but awful" in policing circles—it is not necessarily a crime. The results of this study lend support to the notion that being unarmed does not mean "not dangerous," in some ways explaining why most police officers are not indicted when such a shooting occurs. The study's findings show that when police officers used deadly force during an encounter with an unarmed citizen, the officer or a third person was facing imminent threat of death or serious injury in the vast majority of situations. Moreover, when police officers used force, their actions were almost always consistent with the accepted legal and policy principles that govern law enforcement in the overwhelming proportion of encounters (as measured by indictments).

Noting the dearth of official data on the context of police shooting fatalities, Shane and Swenson call for the U.S. government to compile comprehensive data so researchers and practitioners can learn from deadly force encounters and improve practices. They further recommend that future research on police shootings should examine the patterns and micro interactions between the officer, citizen, and environment in relation to the prevailing law. The unique data and analysis in this book will inform discussions of police use of force for researchers, policymakers, and students involved in criminal justice, public policy, and policing.

**Jon Shane** is an Associate Professor in the Department of Law, Police Science, and Criminal Justice Administration at John Jay College of Criminal Justice. He retired from the Newark Police Department after 20 years at the rank of captain. Professor Shane has published in leading criminal justice and policing journals, including *Crime Science, Journal of Criminal Justice, Justice Quarterly, Policing: An International Journal of Strategies and Management*, and *Police Practice and Research*. He is the author of *What Every Chief Executive Should Know: Using Data to Measure Police Performance* (Looseleaf Law), *Learning from Error: A Case Study in Organizational Accident Theory* (Springer), and *Confidential Informants: A Closer Look at Police Policy* (Springer). His research focuses on issues in police policy and practice, especially use of force; performance management and issues aimed at management and supervision; social disorganization theory, ecology and crime, violent crime; situational crime prevention; and problem-oriented policing.

**Zoë Swenson** is a special investigator with the New York City Department of Investigation, where she investigates corruption, including financial fraud, assault, contraband smuggling, and sex crimes, relating to the New York City Department of Correction. Swenson holds a Master of Arts in criminal justice from John Jay College of Criminal Justice, where she specialized in criminology and deviance. Her research interests are police policy and practice issues, use of force, and situational crime prevention. She is published in leading criminal justice journals including *Journal of Criminal Justice*, where she explored the prevalence and patterns of fatal police shootings by U.S. police between 2015 and 2016.

# Unarmed and Dangerous

Patterns of Threats by Citizens During
Deadly Force Encounters with Police

**Jon Shane and Zoë Swenson**

Routledge
Taylor & Francis Group

NEW YORK AND LONDON

First published 2019
by Routledge
711 Third Avenue, New York, NY 10017

and by Routledge
2 Park Square, Milton Park, Abingdon, Oxon, OX14 4RN

*Routledge is an imprint of the Taylor & Francis Group, an informa business*

© 2019 Taylor & Francis

The right of Jon Shane and Zoë Swenson to be identified as
authors of this work has been asserted by them in accordance with
sections 77 and 78 of the Copyright, Designs and Patents Act 1988.

All rights reserved. No part of this book may be reprinted or
reproduced or utilised in any form or by any electronic, mechanical,
or other means, now known or hereafter invented, including
photocopying and recording, or in any information storage or
retrieval system, without permission in writing from the publishers.

*Trademark notice*: Product or corporate names may be trademarks
or registered trademarks, and are used only for identification and
explanation without intent to infringe.

*Library of Congress Cataloging-in-Publication Data*
A catalog record for this book has been requested

ISBN: 978 1 138 32269 2 (hbk)
ISBN: 978 0 429 44371 9 (ebk)

Typeset in Times New Roman
by Apex CoVantage, LLC

MIX
Paper from
responsible sources
FSC
www.fsc.org    FSC™ C013985

Printed in the United Kingdom
by Henry Ling Limited

# Contents

# Preface

Police use of force, especially deadly force, is always a contentious issue that demands external scrutiny, introspection, and public discourse. Police officers are vested with "powers of the moment" that escape the pensive thought and deliberation reflected in a judge's calm chambers. We expect our police officers to act quickly and decisively to resolve conflict. We summon the police when we are at our worst . . . and we arm them as a means of last resort to stop someone's imminent and escalating threat to our safety. Although we permit police officers to act on our behalf to preserve peace, we do not grant them unfettered authority to do as they please. That would be unreasonable. When a police officer perceives an imminent deadly threat, we expect them to respond in a measured and reasonable manner. While police work certainly entails a degree of risk, we also do not expect police officers to absorb the uncertainty and ambiguity that often pervade policing by requiring them to purposely sacrifice their lives when under attack. That would be unreasonable.

The public debate surrounding police use of deadly force when encountering an unarmed individual often lacks contextual details necessary to make a reasoned judgment about its legality. What dominates the media headlines is a modern-day story of David and Goliath; an underdog (unarmed citizen) set upon by an establishment villain (armed police officer) in a mismatched contest on an uneven playing field. The underdog in American culture is highly regarded. At its core is the Judeo-Christian parable of the warrior who is defeated by his younger adversary, and which serves as the archetypal example of someone who is able to overcome the perceived injustice of such a mismatched contest. The unarmed offender is often lauded as the martyr in this encounter; however, the underdog may just be the unsuspecting police officer who knows not when an attack will launch that will end his or her life.

This research was undertaken to close a gap in the use of force literature and extend our understanding of the type of imminent threat an officer was facing when they killed an unarmed offender. Part of the intent is to dispel the myth that unarmed offenders are not dangerous; therefore, the police officers should not have used deadly force. Underestimating an unarmed offender's skill, ability, or intent when a threat materializes can increase the risk of death or serious bodily injury to a police officer or third party, an outcome too great to bear if a police officer fails to act. A police officer is not required to prevail in their encounter with an offender through a strategy of prayer, hidden wisdom, or happenstance. They get the right to prevail by relying on the authority to act and use force vested in them by the State. Once this happens they are subsequently called to account for their actions. Accountability is not synonymous with punishment; accountability is the willingness to subordinate oneself to a process that requires and expects that person to justify their actions and decisions through official reports, internal investigations, grand jury presentations, prosecutorial review, and criminal trials. Unfortunately, most onlookers believe that if a police officer is not punished for using force against an unarmed person, then they are not held accountable. This too is unreasonable.

Most previous research on police use of force relies on sociodemographic data (age, race, sex, poverty status) to explain relationships between the officer, the offender, and the use of force. While these characteristics may be interesting, they do little if anything to reveal the situational circumstances facing the officer at the moment he or she used force. Reducing the incidence of deadly force should be the overarching concern of researchers and police administrators. Research should help identify the situational correlates of deadly force encounters that can inform tactics, training, and policy development in the way the National War College is concerned with the postwar joint education of the armed forces. Except, reliable national incident-level data are not yet available. The fragmented and decentralized nature of U.S. policing has left policymakers and police executives speculating about what the landscape of deadly force looks like. The

U.S. government has not developed a national incident-based reporting system for deadly force, which leaves open-source data like the *Washington Post* as the default for a nationwide picture on such incidents. Although the *Post* should be lauded for their efforts, the data do not capture all that is needed to learn how to reduce police shootings. Perhaps more importantly, a policy of this sort is the government's responsibility, not a private corporation's responsibility.

Deadly force is an infrequent but critical aspect of policing. Studying the antecedents of every incident is an extension of micro-criminology that can provide rich contextual detail that is absent in macro-criminology. Police administrators and policymakers need more information about the types of encounters that are likely to lead to an attack, which includes attributes of the officer, the offender, and the environment. This study addresses part of that model, but is limited given the data. It does reveal how the armed-unarmed dichotomy fuels fallacious arguments and rancorous debate about an offender's dangerousness, but it stops short of developing an environmental perspective of a police shooting. That domain is nearing and this research is a small window into what we can know and how we can improve officer safety when dealing with unarmed offenders.

**Jon M. Shane**
**Zoë Swenson**

# Foreword

I first met Dr. Shane in 1996 when he was serving as a fellow at the Police Foundation, where I have worked since 1993. Early in my career, I was just completing my PhD in Psychology at George Mason University, while Sergeant Shane was working in the Research and Analysis section in the Newark, New Jersey police department, where we had been completing some work on implementing an early warning system. We had taken a look at some preliminary data, and found that those in the department who had shot dogs were significantly more likely to shoot people, and thus began an ongoing relationship based on mutual interests of human behavior in law enforcement, use of force and less lethal force, ethics, organizational culture, police performance, and a range of issues around stress in policing.

Since those early discussions over 20 years ago, Sergeant Shane became Captain Shane as we continued to discuss the issues around answering important questions in policing. Using data we captured as part of a study on shift work (see Amendola et al., 2011), with his assistance, he examined various stressors (operational and organizational) to complete his doctoral degree at Rutgers; a few years later, he retired from the Newark Police Department and accepted a faculty appointment at John Jay College of Criminal Justice in 2009. I had every confidence at that time that he would achieve his future goals, as he always thought a bit outside the box, while also observing unique aspects of policing not typically the subject of research.

This manuscript is one example of Dr. Shane's "out of the box" thinking and, in some manner, begins to dismantle the broad generalizations associated with police in an era of growing criticism over highly publicized incidents regarding police and citizen encounters, particularly within communities of color. As a psychologist, I can't help sharing in some of the same concerns about the limits of police authority and use of force, the conditions under which force is applied, and the disparate impact of police and justice system procedures on (especially) African-Americans or those of color. But it would be shameful to make generalizations about the behavior of an entire profession based on limited information, and the cloud of scrutiny surrounding that limited information. No doubt, the history of racism in the country is not "all behind us," nor is it fair to expect individuals touched by it (directly or indirectly) to just "get over it." This is not how trauma operates and much of what we know about racial relations in the U.S. involves trauma.

As you will see in Dr. Shane's assessment of data collected by the *Washington Post* and his contextual discussion, the way in which emotionally charged events are presented to the public (usually within some political context depending on the media source) should not substitute for each of our own evaluations based on the facts of the individual cases and the legal boundaries and justifications for police use of deadly force. While most members of the public do not have the same level of research savvy as policing scholars, legal scholars, sociologists, or psychologists, it is not surprising that many interpret such cases within the realm of their own biases, beliefs, or political views (this is unfortunate, but it is human nature). In fact, the same can be said of scientists and researchers, despite our training to be led by scientific objectivity. Indeed, the entirety of facts in every encounter between police and citizens, the vast majority of which do not end in violence or use of force, are rarely available to those of us not involved in the investigations of use of force. As such, most people are without a full understanding of the legal context and standard of "reasonableness" under law, and for that matter, administrative and cultural influences on behavior. As such, we tend to rely on the information we pick up from the media (television, radio, social media, and print, the latter of which often contains more evidentiary facts than the other sources, but is dwindling in readership). Yet, not only are these without biases, but the order in which we receive facts, the way in which they are presented, and the unfortunate tendency of reporters to go beyond reporting and draw conclusions or add commentary without thinking first (as famed journalist Walter Cronkite has suggested) limits our ability to draw accurate conclusions. Such is the age of media outlets today, and while it may be incumbent on each of us to do our own research, the way in which we are expected to when voting in elections in this country, the paid advertisements and unconfirmed statements of fact often lead us to choose expediency over accuracy.

None of this is intended as a criticism of the media, but if anything, a call for greater scrutiny in our perceptions, interpretations, and judgments, lest we will slip into beliefs, as some have, that there is a conspiracy of the entire policing profession (approximately 1.1. million sworn state and local officers as of 2012; Bureau of Justice Statistics, 2016) to systematically target individuals. Unfortunately, at least in my view, ordinary people (including ordinary sworn law enforcement officers) or organizations don't have time or sophistication to orchestrate such a nationwide plot. Further, the policing function in the U.S. is a state matter (except in cases of civil rights law), and is highly localized. And police and sheriffs across the country come from various political viewpoints, so the idea that every one of the 18,000 police departments in the country are engaged in a vast conspiracy is absurd, since it would be virtually impossible to orchestrate. At the same time, culture may allow some individuals to do things that they should not. In the recent and acclaimed film *Three Billboards Outside of Ebbing, MO*, the writer and director make a satirical reference to such abusive police behavior within a very specific and localized cultural context that is dismissive until an African-American Chief takes over, although they demonstrate this improper behavior without subtlety or delicacy, and in an outrageously exaggerated way (or at least I hope so—but you would have to see it to judge for yourself).

You will see throughout this manuscript how a simple classification scheme used by the media (but could just as easily have been by a scholar) can distort the frame within which we interpret data, again demonstrating Dr. Shane's outside the box thinking on this matter. As most scholars learned in graduate school, that there is a way of, well, let's say of misleading (dare I say "lying") with the statistics, those of us charged with researching such matters should also resist the need to perpetuate beliefs and rather deal directly in the realm of facts (including cultural ones, if these can be determined). If nothing else, Dr. Jon Shane has raised doubts about the motivations behind behavior as ones not determined largely by role or culture to a more appropriate focus on each person as an individual by examining each case and its surrounding and unique facts, instead of allowing a shroud of "conspiracy" claims to emotionally escalate the issue of race. Language, bound by its semantics, can be quite powerful, even when well-intentioned people are trying to ascribe meaning. This paper provides an alternative view, although this is not about who is right, the police vs. everyone else (after all the police *are* the people and the people *are* the police); it is about greater understanding by all of us.

**Dr. Karen L. Amendola, PhD,**
*Chief Behavioral Scientist, Police Foundation,*
*Washington, D.C.*
*President of the Division of Experimental Criminology,*
*American Society of Criminology*

# Acknowledgments

The authors wish to acknowledge Ray Hoffman, ESQ, Essex County Prosecutor's Office, Newark, NJ (retired) for his comments on an earlier version of this paper, Dr. Karen L. Amendola, Chief Behavioral Scientist, Police Foundation, Washington, D.C. for her comments and contribution, and the anonymous reviewers who made this a stronger contribution to the literature.

# 1 Introduction

The State's right to use sanctioned violence against its citizens is born of the notion that people give up their individual right of reparation in favor of the State to do their bidding for them (the social contract, Rousseau, 1762/1968). The State legislates on behalf of the individual to avoid a "state of nature," where individual desires and impulses are not tempered by reason and, worst of all, society would live in "continual fear and danger of violent death, and the life of man, solitary, poor, nasty, brutish, and short" (Hobbes, 1651/2012, p. 102). To ensure compliance with its laws, the State designates enforcement agents with a limited set of powers. When an enforcement agent uses force to gain compliance with its laws, the citizenry is understandably concerned since force is arguably the most contentious aspect of government intrusion into personal liberty, upon which democracy is built; as such, police use of force has been a source a political, social, and academic interest dating to at least the 1960s (Harding & Fahey, 1973; Jacobs & Britt, 1979; Kobler, 1975a, 1975b; McEwen, 1996; Robin, 1963; Sherman, 1980; Sherman, Cohn & Gartin, 1986), including the laws and crimes that justify deadly force (Sherman & Langworthy, 1979). When an enforcement agent is believed to act outside their formal authority, the State activates an accountability mechanism that is intended to protect the citizenry from unlawful and oppressive government practices, which reinforces the supremacy of the rule of law over the rule of man.[1]

The Fourth Amendment to the U.S. Constitution protects citizens against unlawful government intrusion (formally known as seizures); any use of force by police must be reasonable in this regard, where reasonable is defined as the balance between the right of the State to have its laws obeyed against the individual's right to be free from unlawful government intrusion (*United States v. Place*, 1983). Before any use of force can be constitutionally permissible, it must be both proportional and immediately necessary. This assessment is context-dependent and idiosyncratic to the location, officer, offender and all of the situational conditions that inform the totality of the circumstances (*Illinois v. Gates*, 1983). The "totality of the circumstances" standard recognizes there is no single determining factor for permissible police action; rather, the judicial system must consider all the facts as they appear to an officer in a given situation and conclude from the whole picture whether probable cause exists (permissible police action), or whether a crime has been committed under color of law (impermissible police action).

Any claim by a citizen that they have been subjected to excessive force—deadly or non-deadly—during the course of an arrest or investigative detention is analyzed under the Fourth Amendment's "objective reasonableness" standard (*Graham v. Connor*, 1989). The *Graham* standard dictates whether the officers' actions are "objectively reasonable" given the facts and circumstances presented to them at the time force was applied and without regard to their underlying intent or motivation. Although the test of reasonableness does not lend itself to a "precise definition or mechanical application" (*Bell v. Wolfish*, 1979), its proper application must be judged from the perspective of a "reasonable officer"[2] (Alpert & Smith, 1994; Terrill, 2009) on the scene, rather than with the "20/20 vision of hindsight," and its calculus embodies an allowance for the fact that police officers are often forced to make split-second decisions about the type and amount of force necessary in a given situation.

Many onlookers do not necessarily understand the law's standard of reasonableness; instead they rely on their personal impressions of reasonableness. Furthermore, media portrayals of police and use of force encounters can negatively influence public sentiment (Pickett et al., 2015); indeed, some organizations and/or individuals are often incensed about how and against whom police officers use force, and they often castigate prosecutors and courts for failing to punish police officers for what they perceive as a criminal act (Bauerlien & McWhirter, 2016; Buckley et al., 2017; Calacal, 2017; Chamberlain, 2017). This reaction suggests that any use of deadly force against an *unarmed* citizen is unreasonable, biased, or unwarranted. The tone of such criticisms is often as vociferous today as it was in the 1960s during the tumultuous civil rights era (Kerner Commission, 1968; Reiss, 1968), although subsequent research suggested that some allegations of police use of excessive force during that period were overstated (Friedrich, 1980).

Nevertheless, the critics' reactions are often facile and predicated on characteristics that do not or should not have any impact on the imminence of a threat, such as a citizen's race (e.g., Calacal, 2017); indeed, several studies on police use of force reveal no identifiable patterns that imply a relationship between an officer's race/ethnicity and an offender's race/ethnicity (Lawton, 2007; McCluskey, Terrill & Paoline, 2005; Morabito & Socia, 2015; Paoline & Terrill, 2005; Phillips & Smith, 2000). In this vacuum of contextual details, an appeal to emotion arises; logic and reasoning are cast aside in favor of personal experience, vicarious anecdotes, and highly sensational incidents that signal a "crisis" or an "epidemic" to political and social pundits. Yet, such media-filtered facts and lack of legal knowledge often appeal to emotion, and may carry more force than reason, individual case facts, judicial processes, and law, but may be fraught with lack of knowledge/information, misinterpretations, or misinformation. Assumptions such as the illegality of a police officer shooting an unarmed citizen frequently lead some to demonize police and demand a federal investigation and/or an independent prosecutor for civil rights violations, despite little understanding of the complexity of the law, or of police training and policies[3] (Barret & Belkin, 2016; Hernandez, 2016; Hernandez & Repart, 2016; Williams, 2016), not to mention the dynamics of each individual case. In cases where the incidents involve (mostly) white officers and unarmed African-American/Black citizens, and the federal government declines to accept the case for investigation, or when they do accept the case and the outcome is not to the public's liking, many deride the criminal justice system as one where African-Americans are "dehumanized" (Goff et al., 2008; Owusu-Bempah, 2016), where whites are implicitly favored (Smith, Levinson & Robinson, 2014), or where police officers tend to hold more implicitly biased[4] views than others in society (Nix et al., 2017; Sidanius et al., 2003). Yet, measuring implicit bias has been heartily criticized by a number of measurement psychologists (see e.g., Brendl, Markman &

Messner, 2001; Fiedler, Messner & Bluemke, 2006) and has demonstrated poor predictive ability (Oswald et al., 2013).[5]

When analyzing real-world shooting data involving working police officers instead of simulated exercises with students or police officers in a controlled/laboratory setting, the findings suggest that Black offenders are not disproportionately the target of police shootings by officers, at least in one Southwestern municipal police department in the United States; Black offenders are approximately one-third as likely to be shot as other offenders (Worrall et al., in press). Similar research involving police officers of the NYPD found that

> Black officers were 3.3 times more likely to shoot than white officers ($p = 0.01$). . . . This finding runs counter to concerns that white officers are overrepresented among officers using lethal force and is consistent with several previous studies of officer race and police use-of-force.
>
> (Ridgeway, 2016, p. 5)

These studies challenge the current bias narrative across the country that White officers are more likely to shoot Black offenders; these studies also counter the narrative that diversity, in and of itself, within police departments relative to the community they serve will make police officers safe (Barrick, Hickman & Strom, 2014). Thus, it is inaccurate to assume all police officers have the same attitudes or intentions, or would take the same actions in the same cases. Hence, focusing specifically on the case characteristics and details may prove a more objective approach to understanding whether outrage is warranted.

Specifically, one area that has not been explored and may reduce misconceptions or inaccurate characterizations of police motives is the dichotomy of an armed vs. unarmed person (a common focus of the media's focus or portrayal of officer-involved shootings), which may present a highly skewed view of the actual level of threat facing the officer when a shooting occurs (MacDonald, 2016). There is a widely held assumption by many in the media and probably others that because a citizen is unarmed, that renders them not dangerous or threatening. In fact, there is no data to support such a conclusion. The very sense of being unarmed connotes an imbalanced encounter, with the citizen at an extreme disadvantage, such as someone walking down the street minding their own business. One of the most vivid symbols of the unarmed defenseless citizen is the fatal shooting of Michael Brown in Ferguson, Missouri on August 9, 2014 (U.S. Department of Justice, 2015). Brown's death galvanized the Black Lives Matter and the "Hands UP. . . . Don't Shoot" movements. By their own account, the Black Lives Matter movement views the world as one where "Black lives are systematically and intentionally targeted for demise."[6] The Malcolm X Grassroots Movement declared "in 2012, police summarily executed more than 313 Black people— one every 28 hours. The use of deadly force against Black people is standard practice in the US—woven into the very fabric of society."[7] This emotionally provocative, broad statement is a conclusion not defended by facts or law.

The actions and rhetoric of some social movements is so highly charged that on August 3, 2017, the FBI assessed that "it is very likely Black Identity Extremist (BIE)[8] perceptions of police brutality against African-Americans spurred an increase in premeditated, retaliatory lethal violence against law enforcement and will very likely serve as justification for such violence" (p. 2).[9] The BIE movement (and some of its violent tendencies) traces its history to the 1960s and 1970s, emerging during the Civil Rights Movement with groups such as the Black Liberation Army who advocated "tak[ing] up arms for the liberation and self-determination of black people in the United States" (Federal Bureau of Investigation, 2017, p. 2). New groups such as the Moorish Sovereign Citizens embrace BIE ideology with a mix of anti-authoritarianism, rejecting U.S. citizenship and believing established, conventional government structures are illegitimate. Although there are certainly instances where police use of force may not be justified, or could have been avoided, the consternation drawn from very limited anecdotes (such as Michael Brown) or selective cases does not reflect the rarity of such events, the totality of circumstances under which they occurred, nor the perceptions of threat assessed by the officers involved.

Threats to the public and to the agents that represent the State manifest in different ways and do not necessarily involve weapons/ firearms. The perceived physical strength of the citizen, an adroit fighter (e.g., boxer; mixed martial artist), a history of mental illness, or level of impairment from alcohol or drugs are just a few contributing factors the courts will examine when assessing what constitutes necessary force vis-a-vis the threat so faced (*Hunt v. County of Whitman*, 2006; *Krueger v. Fuhr*, 1993; *Sharrar v. Felsing*, 1997). In *Sharrar v. Felsing*, the Third Circuit provided additional factors to consider:

> [t]he possibility that the persons subject to the police action are themselves violent or dangerous, the duration of the action, whether the action takes place in the context of effecting an arrest, the possibility that the suspect may be armed, and the number of persons with whom the police officers must contend at one time.[10]

Over 30 years before the *Sharrar v. Felsing* (1997) decision, researchers using data involving Philadelphia police officers discovered that deadly force was most likely to occur when offenders resisted[11] in some manner (Robin, 1963); subsequent research found that offenders who were attacking the officer, resisted in some manner, or were aggressive toward the officer were more likely to have force used against them by the officer (Meyer, 1980; Milton et al., 1977; Worrall et al., in press). Even when a confrontation with a citizen is evenly matched, a police officer is not obligated to retreat or desist; indeed, the officer may stand their ground and press forward to achieve a lawful objective (i.e., effect an arrest), which includes using force to overcome the citizen's actual or threatened resistance. This is true whether the citizen is armed or unarmed.

Society expects police officers to use force judiciously; however, when an officer decides that force is necessary, society also expects the officer will act decisively to protect themselves and other citizens. Police officers are not required to use or to consider alternatives that increase danger to themselves or to others, nor are they required to methodically walk through a series of lesser-force options that delay stopping an imminent threat, or are impractical given the circumstances. Nevertheless, many officers often decide to use a less lethal method, provided it is appropriate or sufficient, and sometimes to their own detriment or demise, perhaps in part due to their concerns over post-incident scrutiny by the public, media, or their own agencies.[12] Indeed, police officers neglect their duty if they unnecessarily delay taking action by performing a ritual of perfunctory force options before arriving at the force option suitable for the circumstance. Instead, police officers are trained to forego unnecessary or impractical force options and escalate to the amount of force commensurate with the force or resistance being offered in order to control the situation (National Institute of Justice, 1999, p. xi). Once the threat has stopped, the officers must deescalate and assess the situation. If force against the officer escalates during the assessment period, then the officer can escalate his or her force to meet that force with reasonable force; if the force against the officer stops, then the officer must stop his or her use of force. A single police-citizen encounter that begins with a mere inquiry may ripen into a deadly force situation in an instant, which prevents an officer from using lesser-force options or taking evasive action (Sykes & Clark, 1975). Some of the most common encounters include initiating traffic stops, investigating crimes, and interacting with potentially dangerous offenders (Hessl, 2003; Tiesman et al., 2010). As such, it is unreasonable and illogical for police officers to delay taking necessary action or deliberately walk through the sequential steps of lesser-force options, thus prolonging the encounter and unnecessarily exposing the officers and the public to further harm.[13] Many myths lead to misunderstandings of these facts (e.g. "officers should shoot suspects in the leg or arm to maim, but not kill,"), something that is neither required by law, nor recommended in any known training programs for reasons outside the scope of this inquiry.

*[handwritten margin note: But what about age of offender (Ex: Tamir rice? (12 years old)]*

Thus, the assumption that unarmed citizens are not dangerous, violent, or threatening is itself dangerous to the lives of officers and the public they are sworn to protect. Labeling a citizen as "unarmed" does not reveal the context of the encounter between the officer and the citizen; between 2006 and 2015, data from the FBI Uniform Crime Report, Law Enforcement Officers Killed and Assaulted show that 24 officers were killed when they were disarmed by citizens.[14] Research supports the notion that offenders who act aggressively toward officers are 29 times more likely to be shot compared to those who do not act aggressively toward officers (Worrall et al., in press), and using force is also more likely when offenders are involved in a violent crime (Alpert, Dunham & MacDonald, 2004; Friedrich, 1980). The

U.S. Supreme Court has never placed absolute restrictions on police use of deadly force to seize an unarmed felon (*Tennessee v. Garner*, 1985). In fact, the Court declared that it is permissible to use deadly force to seize an unarmed suspected felon when it is necessary to prevent an escape and the officer has probable cause to believe that the citizen poses *a significant threat of death or serious physical injury to the officer or others*. Once the encounter meets these conditions, the court examines the totality of the circumstances to assess the reasonableness of the seizure against the three-pronged standard enunciated in *Graham v. Connor* (1989).[15] Whether the citizen is armed or unarmed is merely one aspect of the analysis, and simply because a citizen does not have a physical weapon does not render the person less threatening, nor the seizure unreasonable.

This paper uses publicly available data collected by the *Washington Post* to categorize and describe the threat an officer was facing when the officer used deadly force against an unarmed citizen; the *Post* classified all deadly force encounters as involving either armed or unarmed citizens. In response to this classification, this paper demonstrates that this classification is misleading when context is missing. The federal legal standard for police use of force vis-a-vis the type of encounter/threat the officer was facing (18 U.S.C § 242) more accurately demonstrates the proper characterization of these encounters, as opposed to grouping them into less useful dichotomies, and delineates the elements that must be met before a police officer can be charged with a crime in these cases. The results show that when police officers used deadly force during an encounter with an unarmed citizen, they were facing an imminent threat of death or serious bodily injury[16] to themselves or to a third person in 88.4% of the situations; the remaining 11.6% of the fatalities were due to accidental shootings and unintentional discharges. The results also show that when the officers used force, their actions were consistent with the accepted legal and policy principles that govern use of force in law enforcement in 92.9% of the encounters (as measured by indictments); one case ended with an indictment for a federal civil rights violation.[17] Although any police shooting, even a justified shooting, is not a desired outcome—often termed "lawful but awful" (may have been preventable) in policing circles—it is not necessarily a crime.

# Notes

1 In policing, the right to redress government is operationalized in various ways; internal to the organization that right exists in the internal affairs function, external to the organization that right exists through the prosecutor's office, the state Attorney General's office, the U.S. Attorney's Office (for federal civil rights violations), and judicially through civil lawsuits.
2 A reasonable officer is typically defined as an officer with similar training and experience who, in light of that training and experience, makes a use of force decision that is similar to the decision made by the officer whose decision is in question.
3 In a *Huffington Post* article, Reverend Jesse Jackson characterized Alton Sterling's death involving Baton Rouge police officers as a "legal lynching" (Retrieved on January 20, 2018 from www.huffingtonpost.com/entry/alton-sterling-jesse-jackson-legal-lynching_us_577d126be4b0a629c1ab56c6).
4 The validity of implicit bias tests has been questioned for quite some time and recent research strongly suggests "the statistical evidence is simply too lacking for the [implicit bias] test to be used to predict individual behavior" (Singal, 2017, p. 8; see also Blanton, Jaccard & Burrows, 2015; James, Klinger & Vila, 2014; Oswald et al., 2013, 2015).
5 Also see Johnson (May, 2017) for factual examination of the empirical evidence surrounding the concept of implicit bias, implicit bias tests, and the relationship between implicit bias test scores and actual discriminatory behavior.
6 Retrieved on June 20, 2017 from http://blacklivesmatter.com/guiding-principles/.
7 Retrieved on June 20, 2017 from https://mxgm.org/wp-content/uploads/2013/05/we-charge-genocide-FINAL.pdf. The data source is not identified.
8 Black Identity Extremism is defined by the FBI as "individuals who seek, wholly or in part, through unlawful acts of force or violence, in response to perceived racism and injustice in American society and some do so in furtherance of establishing a separate black homeland or autonomous black social institutions, communities, or governing organization within the United States. This desire for physical or psychological separation is typically based on either a religious or political belief system, which is sometimes formed around or includes a belief in racial superiority or supremacy" (FBI Intelligence Assessment, Black Identity Extremists Likely Motivated to Target Law Enforcement Officers, p. 2; Retrieved on October 10, 2017 from https://assets.documentcloud.org/documents/4067711/BIE-Redacted.pdf). The FBI acknowledges that "the mere advocacy of violent tactics may not constitute extremism, and may be constitutionally protected" (p. 2).
9 FBI Intelligence Assessment, Black Identity Extremists Likely Motivated to Target Law Enforcement Officers; Retrieved on October 10, 2017 from https://assets.documentcloud.org/documents/4067711/BIE-Redacted.pdf.
10 *Santini v. Fuentes,* 795 F.3d 410, 417 (3d Cir. 2015) (citing *Sharrar v. Felsing,* 128 F.3d 810, 822 (3d Cir. 1997)). Previous research also shows that as the number of bystanders increases, so too does the likelihood of arrest, particularly in public places (Friedrich, 1980). This is likely related to the control function of policing, insofar as officers will effect an arrest to assert their position as a show of authority to preempt any further disorder or violence.

11  Actions that are synonymous with resisting include combat, confront, defy, prevent, refuse, repel, thwart, assail, assault, battle, duel, hinder, persist, fight back, hold off, keep from, put up a fight, stand up to, and struggle against. None of these terms suggest someone must be armed before resistance is offered.

12  One vivid example is a widely-reported incident involving a Chicago police officer who was facing an imminent deadly threat from an unarmed attacking offender, but chose not to respond with deadly force because she was concerned about post-incident scrutiny (Retrieved on January 20, 2018 from http://abc7chicago.com/news/chicago-cop-says-she-feared-using-gun-while-being-beaten/1543015/; www.chicagotribune.com/news/local/breaking/ct-citing-beating-of-officer-chicago-s-top-cop-says-police-are-second-guessing-them-selves-20161006-story.html; www.cbsnews.com/news/chicago-police-say-officer-didnt-shoot-during-beating-fearing-scrutiny/).

13  See *McLenagan v. Karnes*, 27 F.3d 1002, 4th Cir. 1994, at 1007, where the court acknowledged in certain circumstances "warnings," which are tantamount to the lesser-force options, may not be feasible and thus are not necessarily required prior to using deadly force. In *Tennessee v. Garner* (1985) the Court suggested a warning should precede the use of force, but did not make this principle compulsory.

14  FBI UCR, 2015 Law Enforcement Officers Killed and Assaulted, Table 19. Retrieved on June 20, 2017 from https://ucr.fbi.gov/leoka/2015/tables/table_19_leos_fk_vo_killed_with_own_weapon_disarmed_of_weapon_and_weapon_stolen_by_citizen_2006-2015.xls.

15  The three-prong *Graham* standard is: 1) the severity of the crime at issue; 2) whether the suspect poses an immediate threat to the safety of the officers or others; and 3) whether he is actively resisting arrest or attempting to evade arrest by flight (see *Tennessee v. Garner*, 471 U.S., pp. 8–9, where the operative questions is: "whether the totality of the circumstances justifie[s] a particular sort of . . . seizure").

16  Serious bodily injury is generally defined as bodily injury which creates a substantial risk of death or which causes serious, permanent disfigurement, or protracted loss or impairment of the function of any bodily member or organ (e.g., N.J.S.A. 2C:11–1, Definitions).

17  Death of Walter Scott by Officer Michael Slager, North Charleston, SC police department. Officer Slager pleaded guilty to federal civil rights violations on May 2, 2017 (Yan, Shah & Grimberg, 2017).

# 2    Focal Concerns of Police Officers and the Legal Framework

## Threats to a Police Officer

Generally, a threat is "an expression of intention to inflict evil, injury, or damage . . . an indication of something impending,"[1] which may be expressed verbally or through actions, and is synonymous with terms such as danger and risk. Threats to police officers manifest through a combination of three characteristics that shape the encounter: 1) the citizen; 2) the officer; and the 3) environment (Binder & Scharf, 1980; Holmes et al., 1998; Wheeler et al., in press; Worden, 1989). When these situational characteristics converge they create the opportunity structure for a threat to develop and manifest in the officer's mind, sometimes referred to as the "deadly mix" (Pinizzotto et al., 2012). Cognition, perception, and human emotion play a role in every-day life (Pichon, de Gelder & Grezes, 2012), and in the life of a police officer those tendencies are shaped by training, work experiences, and vicarious experiences with other officers. Threats often develop at close range with citizens, such as during a foot pursuit, a field interview, or a physical fight (Petersson et al., 2017). Research demonstrates there is a negative correlation between the threat and physical distance, i.e., that as distance increases the perceived threat decreases (Stamps, 2012); said differently, as distance decreases, perceived threat increases.

Similar research examined whether stimuli that appear to be closer are more threatening. Stimuli that emit affective signals of threat (e.g., an aggressive male student) were perceived as physically closer than stimuli that emit affective signals of disgust (e.g., a repulsive male student) or no affective signal. When controlling for the direct effects of physiological arousal, object familiarity, and intensity of the negative emotional reaction, the study also showed that threatening stimuli appeared to be physically closer than disgusting stimuli (Cole, Balcetis & Dunning, 2013). A separate study involving police officers explored the impact of threat on distance perception and behavior (Nieuwenhuys, Cañal-Bruland & Oudejans, 2012). Armed police officers were presented with threatening stimuli, the hypotheses being that in threatening situations, distance judgments would not be as accurate in low-threat circumstances. Two groups of officers were compared, those in the actual response group and those in the verbal response group. Both groups were presented with low-threat stimuli (a man with a plastic knife) and high-threat stimuli (a man with an electric knife). When the approaching man failed to respond to the officers' orders to stop, he was shot. The results showed that high-threat situations led to earlier shooting in the actual response group. This suggests that anxiety changes the relationship between distance and perceived threat. Stated differently, threatening stimuli will appear closer than nonthreatening stimuli, which has implications for tactics, approach, and reaction time.

Other studies show that active, sworn police officers across the United States are remarkably restrained when facing a threat where they could have legally used deadly force, but decided not to do so. In one study, officers reported exercising restraint in 93% of the situations in which they could have legally fired their weapon, but did not do so (Pinizzotto et al., 2012), and another study showed that officers did not respond with deadly force at the earliest possible moment when they could have; rather, they waited for "a very clear indication of suspect intentions" (Doerner, 1991, p. 8), which in some cases could be fatal to an officer.

Even when citizens may appear to be in-custody or subdued and under control as they lie in a prone position, they can still threaten a police officer with remarkable speed. One study examined the dangerousness of a citizen in the prone position compared to the speed at which an individual with "hidden hands" can fire a weapon. The results show that citizens can fire a weapon from the initial movement of any body part to discharge in a little over half a second[2] and the time from first object sighting (noting something in the citizen's hand) to discharge was approximately one-third of a second[3] (Lewinski et al., 2016). The implication is that witnesses who observe a citizen lying prone on the ground who appears not to pose a threat, or appears under control or in custody, can launch an assault exceptionally quickly (see

Blair et al., 2011, where the findings showed that the officers were generally not able to react and to fire before the suspect was able to do so, an action vs. reaction scenario). A separate study comprised of both deadly force incidents and situations in which a shooting could reasonably have been expected, but did not occur, showed that deadly force situations, more so than averted shooting situations, are characterized by ambiguity and surprise (Fridell & Binder, 1992).

The ambiguity, surprise, and uncertainty of a police-citizen encounter is the leeway the U.S. Supreme Court grants officers when facing an imminent threat; this is reflected in the Court's command that judicial analysis be undertaken without the benefit of 20/20 hindsight vision (*Graham v. Connor*, 1989). Virtually every assault against an officer consigns that officer to reaction, which is necessarily defensive and slower than the citizen's offensive action due to visual and auditory recognition that a threat exists. This places police officers at a disadvantage during the encounter by imposing an inherent lag-time constraint upon them; only the citizen knows whether and when he or she will strike. The officers must assess the nature and imminence of the threat by interpreting statements they hear and actions they see or do not see, coupled with contextual factors (e.g., environment, training, experience, expectations), then implement an appropriate and timely response "in direct proportion to the accuracy of their perception of the threat level" (Pinizzotto, Davis & Miller, 2006, p. 76).

Studies involving offenders who have assaulted police officers show that during their violent encounter with the officer, the offender believed the officer did not perceive the seriousness of the threat as it was unfolding until it was too late; officers involved in the same encounter reported that "they were unaware of the impending assault," meaning they did not recognize and react to the threat quickly enough to mitigate the assault (Pinizzotto, Davis & Miller, 2006, p. 3). Underreacting or failing to react to perceived threats, or misperceiving or under-emphasizing an actual threat, may result in death or serious bodily injury to the officer (Clines, 1993; Pinizzotto, Davis & Miller, 2000; see also Doerner, 1991, p. 8 for officer hesitation, accuracy of shot placement, and officer death resulting from late unholstering of their firearm during a simulated shoot/don't shoot exercise).

An officer who reacts to a citizen's verbal and physical gestures implies that it is the citizen who is controlling the officer's response (Gillespie, Hart & Boren, 1998). Police officers are customarily trained to react to telltale signs of danger from a citizen (e.g., hands in pockets or obscured from view, reaching around inside a vehicle or under a seat, agitation or nervousness, inconsistent or conflicting answers to questions, flight from the officer,[4] uncooperativeness, physically charging or running toward the officer, assuming a fighting stance or a firing stance, verbal cues forecasting assault), and when they are confronted with risky, unpredictable, and rapidly evolving situations, where the end point is not known, it is reasonable for them to use force to defend themselves, other officers, and the general public from potential harm. These studies highlight the importance of action versus reaction, time, and distance to slow the operational tempo of an encounter and the officer's ability to successfully navigate the environment.

Threats develop in many ways and the phenomenon is highly complex, consisting of thousands of potential combinations[5] that may become apparent in just seconds, although just a few combinations of circumstances are needed for a deadly threat to materialize. Preparing for such an encounter is a difficult task since replicating real-world life-threatening circumstances in a safe environment can only be simulated so far; police work is often unpredictable and dangerous, which makes it difficult to fully plan for every eventuality or contingency in advance (Lyons et al., 2017), and the danger, stress, and exhaustion of a true deadly threat cannot be replicated in a training environment. Threat modeling, for example, is a training technique used to identify threats from the attacker's perspective. The purpose is to provide police officers with an understanding of how and when an assault may occur so the officer can take preemptive action to either avoid it or mitigate its impact; the doctrine of preemption is fundamental to diffusing hostile or violent encounters and if neither of these is possible, then police officers must develop a plan to confront it, sometimes by using force. Police departments use firearms training simulators (FATS),[6] simulated training ammunition,[7] and simulated tactical environments[8] to model how threats during use of force encounters may occur in real-world settings (Bennell & Jones, 2005; Doerner, 1991; Ho, 1994).

The most obvious threat to an officer involves weaponry, including vehicles. When a citizen is armed and confronts a police officer, the likelihood that the threat will escalate more quickly is apparent. Although assaults involving weapons are most dangerous, unarmed assaults are much more prevalent. The FBI Uniform Crime Report, Law Enforcement Officer Killed and Assaulted (LEOKA) data for 2015 show that officers working alone (24.5%) or working alone but assisted by another officer (37.8%) were more likely to be assaulted while responding to an incident than a two-officer vehicle (17.7%).[9] The 2015 LEOKA data show that 79.0% of assaults against officers occurred from "personal weapons" (i.e., hands, fists, or feet), compared to firearms (4.0%), knives or other cutting instruments (1.8%), and other deadly weapons (15.1%). The same data also show that between 2006 and 2015, officers who sustained an injury from personal weapons steadily increased from 28.4% (2006) to 30.5% (2015). [10]

More recent research involving police officers who were on-duty estimated that between 2003 and 2014 approximately 669,100 law enforcement officers were treated in U.S. emergency rooms for nonfatal injuries. The overall rate of 635 per 10,000 full-time officers was three times higher than all other U.S. workers (213 per 10,000 full-time employed).[11] The leading injury category was assaults and violent acts (35%), with injury rates highest for younger officers (aged 21–24 years) and similar rates for both male and female officers. Rates for assault-related injuries increased for officers between 2003 and 2011 with large and significant increases that started in 2008 and continued through 2012 (Tiesman et al., 2018). Although weapons, particularly firearms, produce more lethal outcomes than personal weapons, the data show that assaults from unarmed citizens are much more frequent and, thus, present a greater risk of occurring.[12] Statistically speaking, given the high percentage of assaults from personal weapons, it is reasonable to expect that a certain percentage of encounters by police with unarmed citizens, albeit small, will end in a shooting.

## Legal Standard for Use of Force

### *Federal Statutory Law*

Police use of force is governed by three principles: 1) statutory law; 2) case law; and 3) agency policy. Although police officers are subject to varying state statutes relating to use of force in law enforcement as well as the outcomes associated with its use (e.g., aggravated assault, murder, manslaughter, aggravated manslaughter, official misconduct), federal statutory and case law are consistent across the United States, which provides uniformity for evaluation purposes. The federal criminal statute that governs use of force by all police officers is 18 U.S.C. § 242 (Deprivation of Rights Under Color of Law). The statute reads, in part:

> Whoever, under color of any law, statute, ordinance, regulation, or custom, willfully subjects any person in any State, Territory, Commonwealth, Possession, or District to the deprivation of any rights, privileges, or immunities secured or protected by the Constitution or laws of the United States. . . [commits a crime].

Although criminal statutes may appear sound, words have meaning and often require a certain degree of interpretation to translate ambiguous language and to ensure constitutionality, which is, admittedly, a moving target. Words are imperfect symbols used to convey expectations and intent; words that appear in criminal statutes such as "may," "reasonably," and "prudent" are permissive, which imply a degree of discretion and which do not command action or omission such as the words "must" or "shall." Consequently, courts must rule on whether the behavior exhibited by a police officer is legal. It is difficult to mathematize the human experience, and unforeseen circumstances and situations are inevitable. As society evolves, so do standards of decency, culture, technology, and new exceptions to the law, which were not anticipated when the legislation was originally crafted. This makes applying statutory standards difficult in some cases. Therefore, the judiciary is tasked with determining how a statute should be enforced through their interpretation. Judicial interpretation can drastically alter the legal landscape, and, in the case of a U.S. Supreme Court decision, the interpretation becomes the law of the land, applicable to all police agencies in the United States (e.g., *Graham v. Connor*, 1989; *Tennessee v. Garner*, 1985).

### Case Law

Case law from the U.S. Supreme Court and the district circuit courts provide police officers with a framework for applying force when necessary and investigating claims of excessive force when they are raised. In 1985, the U.S. Supreme Court declared that a Tennessee state statute that allowed police officers to seize an unarmed, nondangerous fleeing felon by shooting the felon dead was unconstitutional (*Tennessee v. Garner*, 1985; see Tennenbaum, 1994, for the for the influence of the *Garner* decision of police use of deadly force). The Court, however, crafted an exception that deadly force may be used to prevent an escape when the officer has probable cause to believe that the citizen poses a significant threat of death or serious bodily injury to the officer or to others. The *Garner* exception is not predicated on whether the citizen is armed; rather, it is the degree of threat posed by the citizen, which triggers the justification.

Although the *Garner* decision clarified when police can use deadly force in the face of an imminent threat, the Court fell short of explaining how to objectively evaluate that use of force as reasonable or excessive. The Fourth Amendment "reasonableness" inquiry is whether a police officer's actions are "objectively reasonable" given the facts and circumstances confronting an officer at that moment, without regard for their intent or ulterior motives. The "reasonableness" of a particular use of force is assessed from the perspective of an officer on the scene at the moment he or she uses force, with an allowance for the fact that police officers will often make split-second decisions about the quantum of force necessary in a given situation (*Scott v. United States*, 1978).

In *Graham v. Connor* (1989), the U.S. Supreme Court created a three-prong test to assess the objectivity of the officer's actions: 1) the severity if the crime; 2) whether the citizen poses an immediate threat to the safety of the officers or others; and 3) whether the citizen is actively resisting arrest or attempting to evade arrest by flight. The *Graham* test removes the element of subjectivity insofar as an officer's good faith effort when using force does not make an unreasonable seizure reasonable, nor does bad faith make a reasonable seizure unreasonable (*United States v. Robinson*, 1973). Thus, the subjective motivations of individual officers have no bearing on whether a given seizure is unreasonable under the Fourth Amendment. Rather, the threat that occasions the need for deadly force and its subsequent reasonableness determination are examined by the totality of the circumstances (*Illinois v. Gates*, 1983). This means, as a matter of public accountability, the officer is required to articulate specific facts and the inferences drawn from those facts to demonstrate why he or she believed it was necessary to resort to deadly force at that moment. When the facts and circumstances ripen into probable cause—the linchpin of the Fourth Amendment—a police officer will likely prevail in their justification. A citizen's claim they were subjected to excessive force is also analyzed against the *Graham* standard and is not defined by the outcome of a use of force encounter (i.e., injury or death); rather, the necessity, imminence, and proportionality at the time the officer applied force are the driving factors for an unconstitutional claim.

### Police Policy

Statutory law and case law on use of force are embedded in police policies to ensure police agencies adopt contemporary practices consistent with the current state of the law and constitutional principles. Individual police agencies codify operating practices in policies, then promulgate those policies to provide direction and to ensure all personnel are operating within accepted industry standards. A written policy provides officers and supervisors with guidance and direction on the legal and ethical limits governing the practice, specifically acts and omissions, which is intended to increase accountability and consistency in action while concurrently reducing employee autonomy and discretion and improving police performance (Alpert & Dunham, 1992; Alpert & Smith, 1994; American Bar Association, 1980, standards 1–4.2, 1–4.3; Auten, 1988; Goldstein, 1967; Kutzke, 1980; O' Loughlin, 1990; Walker, 2010, pp. 46–49, discussing the potential benefits of confining discretion to promote accountability; Welsh & Harris, 2004, pp. 131–136). Regarding the absence of policy, policing experts note:

> To do otherwise is to simply leave employees "in the dark" in the expectation that they will intuitively divine the proper and expected course of action in the performance of their duties. . . . Discretion must be reasonably exercised within the parameters of the expectations of the community, the courts, the legislature and the organization, itself.
>
> (Auten, 1988, pp. 1–2)

Policy guides decision-making by recognizing that as risk increases, discretion decreases. To ensure accountability, important decisions must be either non-discretionary, or must be limited, meaning the policy must limit police officers' and supervisors' discretion. Research on administrative policy as a means to control police discretion spans a diverse body of academic literature, including police use of deadly force (Fyfe, 1979, 1988; White, 2001); response to domestic violence (Eitle, 2005; Sherman & Berk, 1984); bias crimes (Jenness & Grattet, 2005; King, 2007); DWI enforcement (Mastrofski & Ritti, 1992; Mastrofski, Ritti & Hoffmaster, 1987; Mastrofski, Ritti & Snipes, 1994); and racial profiling (Schultz & Withrow, 2004) among the many. Previous research shows that more restrictive use of force policies result in a decrease in the number of deadly police shootings and in racial disparity (Fyfe, 1979, 1988; White, 2001); the same holds for less-lethal use of force (Terrill & Paoline, 2017).

In this regard, policy is an expression of the will of the public. Without a policy, the agency cuts itself off from the public, where there is a tendency to function with unfettered discretion and outside legal and ethical bounds until individual or collective actions are exposed through scandal, judicial intervention, civil litigation, or government investigation that necessitates reform. Similarly, failure to promulgate or enforce an existing policy is a policy of acquiescence and is tantamount to failing to act—tacit agreement of sorts that the current state of affairs is acceptable. Comprehensive policy is an expression of how the agency intends to conduct its affairs and act in specific situations to minimize liability and errors at the agency, supervisory, and line level, particularly when legal and ethical issues arise. One of the principal reasons police practitioners, policymakers, and the public concern themselves with designing and promulgating policy is because it represents one of the primary tools through which problematic police behavior (individually and collectively as an organization) and complex situations can be controlled and improved. Without guidance from policy, officers do not have uniform procedures to follow, which invites deviance, inconsistency, and misconduct. When police misconduct does occur, it often originates with a failure to design and promulgate a clear written policy; misconduct is also likely to occur from failing to observe a published policy.

The International Association of Chiefs of Police (IACP), law enforcement's leading professional and advocacy group, promulgates the national model policy on use of force.[13] The policy is consistent with U.S. Supreme Court decisions on use of force (i.e., *Graham v. Connor*, 1989; *Tennessee v. Garner*, 1985), but it also sets a baseline under which police agencies should not fall. Since policing is highly variable across the United States, local conditions (i.e., culture, budget constraints, training standards, agency size, degree of urbanization, population density) often impose higher standards on police officers when using force, which gives police agencies the flexibility to meet the demands of the community; nothing prevents a police agency from adopting stricter policies and standards for police practices than those imposed by the courts (Gain, 1971; Fridell, Faggiani, Taylor, Brito & Kubu, 2009; Reiss, 1980; Terrill & Paoline, 2017; White, 2001).[14]

## Legal Standard to Sustain a Conviction for Deprivation of Rights Under Color of Law

When a police officer uses force, they essentially violate the law. Although police officers are subject to state laws for assault, homicide, and official misconduct if they use force unlawfully, one of the most significant crimes they face is depriving someone of their civil rights. Under federal law, to obtain a conviction for deprivation of civil rights under color of law (18 U.S.C. § 242), the prosecution must prove beyond a reasonable doubt that: 1) the police officer was acting under color of law; 2) that he or she acted willfully; 3) that he or she deprived the citizen of a right protected by the Constitution or laws of the United States; and 4) that the deprivation resulted in bodily injury or death. In cases of an arrest (technically termed a seizure resulting from deadly force), the constitutional right at stake for the citizen is governed by the Fourth Amendment's "objectively reasonable" standard, which relies on the facts and circumstances known to the officer at the time he or she used force (*Loch v. City of Litchfield*, 2012; *Nelson v. County of Wright*, 1998). Establishing a police officer's intent behind a Constitutional violation is that he or she acted "willfully" and requires proof that the officer acted with the purpose "to deprive a person of a right which has been made specific either by the express terms of the Constitution or laws of the United States or by decisions interpreting them" (*United States v. Lanier*, 1997). This means a police officer *must know* that what he or she is doing is wrong and continue doing it despite their knowledge (*Screws v. United States*, 1945). This also means the officer must be correct about the law, but may be mistaken about the facts known at the moment; mistakes, misperception, or bad judgment by a police officer using force does not provide the basis for prosecution under Section 242 (*United States v. McClean*, 1976).[15]

When a police officer is on-duty and exhibiting evidence of his or her authority (e.g., attired in uniform, driving a marked police car, displaying a badge, announcing themselves as a police officer), they are acting under color of law. Thereafter, whether a crime occurs from the officer's use of force rests on whether there is sufficient evidence to establish that the force used was unreasonable given the facts and circumstances known to the officer at the time force was applied, and if so, whether the officer acted with "willful"[16] criminal intent to deprive the citizen of a constitutionally protected right. To fulfill that requirement, the prosecutor must present proof that the officer used force under conditions that no other reasonable officer would have perceived as an imminent threat at that moment. If the prosecutor can satisfy this requirement, then an indictment and conviction may attach; if not, then the officer's conduct is justified under the statute. The government must prove that the officer intended to engage in the specific conduct that violated the Constitution and that he or she did so knowing it was a wrongful act. This activates the totality of the circumstance requirement to determine willful behavior and includes consistency in the officers' and witnesses' account of the event, as well as the corroborating physical, documentary, and testimonial evidence from the scene. Evidence regarding the propriety of the officer's conduct, its character and duration, the weapons employed, and the provocation, if any, are also highly relevant to the analysis.

When a police officer intends to use force against someone because of a perceived threat, the government must prove the officer's version of the events is not true. If there is no credible evidence to refute the officer's belief that he or she was acting in self-defense, or defense of a third person—or, stated differently, if there is sufficient credible evidence to support the officer's claim of self-defense or defense of a third person—then a prosecution is not warranted. Even if a police officer is mistaken in their interpretation of the citizen's behavior, or if other witnesses interpret that behavior in the same way as the officer, this would preclude a determination that the officer acted with the purpose to violate the law.

## General Principles of Justification

State and federal criminal codes allow an affirmative defense for conduct that would otherwise be a crime. Necessity is one such justification. To establish necessity, a police officer must articulate the facts and circumstances that he or she committed a crime (i.e., used force against someone) because of pressure from natural forces (i.e., actions from the citizen). The police officer must establish that he or she believed their conduct was necessary to avoid some harm against society that would be greater than the harm caused by his or her criminal conduct (i.e., their use of force). For a police officer's use of force to be necessary, generally four elements must be met:

1   There must be a perception (reasonable and genuine on the part of the actor) of threatened harm;
2   That threatened harm must have arisen through no fault on the part of the actor;[17]
3   The only way to avoid the harm is by committing a criminal act; and
4   The harm threatened is so great that as a matter of public policy it can be said to outweigh the values protected by the criminal law which is broken (Cannel, 2017, p. 180).

Police officers must possess a reasonable belief that force is necessary. It is the belief, not the actual necessity that is important. If necessity exists, but the officer does not believe it, then there is no defense. However, if there is belief without actual necessity, then the first step toward justification is taken. Second, the officer's belief must be reasonable, which is measured objectively; reasonable belief is judged in light of all the facts and circumstances facing the officer at the time when force was applied, irrespective of the officer's ulterior motives or misinterpretations. As some courts have noted, "Detached reflection cannot be demanded in the presence of an uplifted knife" (*Brown v. United States*, 1921); however, it is clear that the facts and circumstances confronting the officer must convey some sense of imminence[18] necessitating the use of force. Restated, this means police officers must be correct about the law (i.e., they have a legal right to use force at the time), but they can be mistaken about the facts (i.e., they shoot someone whom they reasonably believed to be armed, but who was not armed). Fear, for example, is an emotional response to a perceived threat that causes changes in behavior such as whether an officer will stand their ground during an encounter (confront) or withdraw (flee). But fear alone is not sufficient to establish imminence and necessity. Fear must not derive from a phobia or irrational circumstance; there must be some objective circumstance or overt act apart from the officer's subjective perception that arouses fear. Unreasonable fear includes overreaction to a genuine threat, as well as reaction to an artificial threat based on individual prejudice, phobia, or poor application of past experiences. If the officer's fear is not sufficient to cause a reasonable officer to draw the same conclusion, then the officer's actions will not be justified. Although accidental shootings and unintentional discharges may negate culpability, a degree of negligence may be involved, which triggers criminal liability. Prosecution for negligence may attach when a police officer fires their weapon because of operator error, or from poor attention to basic safety rules.[19]

That the facts and circumstances of an encounter must convey some sense of urgency is reflected in the imminence standard. A police officer is justified in using force in self-defense, or defense of a third person, provided that force is necessary during the present occasion. If the threat never materializes, then force is not authorized. Similarly, when the threat has ended, so too must the application of force. It was the final few strikes to motorist Rodney King by Los Angeles police officers on March 3, 1991 as he lay in a prone position that led to criminal liability (*United States v. Koon*, 1993); once King no longer presented a threat, the use of force was not justified, but until that time the officers acted reasonably and consistent with the Fourth Amendment, notwithstanding that King was unarmed.

When necessity and imminence are present, probable cause exists, and when a police officer has probable cause they may use force— including deadly force—in a constitutionally permissible manner

\
Examples of
present day
Tamir rice; Mike Brown

(*Deluna v. City of Rockford*, 2006, citing *Scott v. Edinburg*, 2003; *Nelson v. County of Wright*, 1998; *O'Bert v. Vargo*, 2003; *Tennessee v. Garner*, 1985). Once probable cause exists and a police officer uses force, proportionality is also required. Proportionality is the corresponding type, degree, and duration of force applied by a police officer compared to the type, degree, and amount of resistance offered by the citizen. Proportionality is generally established through an ordinal scale of incremental force options that corresponds to the level of force and resistance encountered, often termed a use of force continuum (e.g., National Institute of Justice, 1999, p. 37). Proportionality of force does not require officers to use the same type or amount of force as the citizen, essentially an equal amount of force. As the threat becomes more pronounced through imminency and more likely to cause death or serious bodily injury, a greater level of force may be applied and will be considered objectively reasonable and necessary as a counter measure. Police officers are not, however, required to use the least intrusive degree of force possible; they are only required to select a reasonable option based on the facts as they know them and from the perspective of a reasonable officer at the scene (*Forrester v. City of San Diego*, 1994).[20] Every time a police officer uses force, the necessity, imminence, and proportionality requirements are invoked. These standards provide police supervisors and prosecutors with an investigative framework to establish objective reasonableness as it relates to the Fourth Amendment. The standards also provide a framework for assessing excessive force (*Payne v. Pauley*, 2003; *United States v. Dykes*, 2005); a police officer is not authorized to use more force than that which he or she reasonably believes is necessary to repel the threat. Restated, the force used by the officer need not be equal to the force used by the citizen, only proportionate to what the officer reasonably believes is necessary.

## Duty to Retreat

Police officers not only have the statutory right to self-defense, but as they execute their public duty they also are conferred with specific rights accorded to their office. While a citizen may have an obligation to retreat in certain states if they can do so safely before they resort to using force, a police officer has no such duty. Even if a police officer's actions are not lawful (e.g., effecting an unlawful arrest), the citizen is compelled to submit to the officer's orders. Most states do not provide an affirmative defense to prosecution by allowing a person to resist an unlawful arrest.[21] In this regard, society expects a police officer to stand their ground and press forward when enforcing the law, and when they are met with resistance to use their knowledge, skills, and abilities to achieve their lawful objective.

## Notes

1  Retrieved on June 21, 2017 from www.merriam-webster.com/dictionary/threat.
2  Mean speed 0.61 seconds.
3  Mean speed 0.36 seconds.
4  Some courts have noted that "unprovoked flight upon noticing the police" is suspicious behavior and that "headlong flight—wherever it occurs—is the consummate act of evasion: It is not necessarily indicative of wrongdoing, but it is certainly suggestive of such" (*Illinois v. Wardlow*, 2000). Other cases have recognized that "nervous [and] evasive behavior is a pertinent factor in determining reasonable suspicion" *United States* v. *Brignoni Ponce* (1975); *Florida v. Rodriguez* (1984).
5  To illustrate the complexity of a police shooting, author Shane conceptualized the interaction between the officer's actions ($n=37$) and the citizen's actions ($n=24$), in relation to the environment ($n=9$). Shane conservatively estimates there are 54,740 unique combinations of threat conditions that could arise. A combination, not a permutation, is the number of ways to choose a sample of $r$ elements from a set of $n$ distinct objects, where the order does not matter and replacements are not permitted.

$$C(n, r) = C(70,3)$$

$$\frac{70!}{(3!(70-3)!)}$$

$$= 54,740$$

6  See one example known as LasarShot Simulations. Retrieved on June 26, 2017 from www.lasershot.com/?gclid=Cj0KEQjw4cLKBRCZmNTvyovvj-4BEiQAl_sgQrFp3sNcycddjq6tWZJ6fesz-rkBw38Oa-beFoEwHK4aAi1w8P8HAQ. Another is MILO/RANGE. Retrieved on December 11, 2017 from www.faac.com/milo-range/.
7  See one example known as Simunition. Retrieved on June 26, 2017 from http://simunition.com/en/.
8  See one example known as Hogan's Alley operated by the FBI at their training facility in Quantico, Virginia. Retrieved on June 26, 2017 from www.fbi.gov/services/training-academy/hogans-alley.
9  Retrieved on June 21, 2017 from https://ucr.fbi.gov/leoka/2015/tables/table_74_leos_asltd_circum_at_scene_of_incident_by_type_of_assignment_and_percent_distribution_2015.xls, Table 74. Also see Kaminski & Marvell (2002) and Austin, Proescholdbell & Norwood (2015) for a discussion of police occupational fatalities resulting from injuries sustained during an assault by a suspect or criminal offender.
10  Retrieved on June 21, 2017 from https://ucr.fbi.gov/leoka/2015/tables/table_75_leos_asltd_type_of_weapon_and_percent_injured_2006-2015.xls, Table 75.
11  Other research on risk factors for workplace violence shows that seven of the ten indicators are applicable to the law enforcement occupation with nearly 60% of primary wounds in fatal assaults coming from head, neck, or throat injuries and

nearly 50% of primary wounds in nonfatal assaults coming from the arms/hands or below the waist (Crifasi, Pollack & Webster, 2016).

12  Retrieved on June 21, 2017 from https://ucr.fbi.gov/leoka/2015/tables/table_28_leos_fk_type_of_weapon_2006-2015.xls, Table 28.

13  See National Consensus Policy on Use of Force, IACP, January 2017, p. 3, Use of Deadly Force.

14  The Police Executive Research Forum (PERF), a leading police research group, issued *Guiding Principles on Use of Force* (March 2016), which suggested that policing could impose higher standards on use of force above that which the U.S. Supreme Court requires.

15  *United States v. McClean* (1976) notes that inadvertence or a mistake negates willfulness for purposes of 18 U.S.C. § 242. Homicide by misadventure—where a police officer, engaged in a lawful action without any intent to injure, kills someone—is an example of negating willfulness.

16  The U.S. Supreme Court has interpreted a willful act as one which is "committed" either "in open defiance or in reckless disregard of a constitutional requirement which has been made specific or definite" (*Screws v. United States*, 1945).

17  Fault, as used here, is legal fault. A police officer is not precluded from using deadly force when warranted due to faults involving tactics, agency policy, or some sort of state-created danger (see Neyfakh, 2015; Noble & Alpert, 2015, pp. 567–582).

18  Imminent means "likely to happen without delay" (American Heritage Dictionary of the English Language, 1996, p. 903). Imminent does not mean instantaneous. Imminent, or imminent danger, describes threatened actions or outcomes that may occur during an encounter independent of a police officer's actions. For example, imminent danger may exist if: 1) an officer reasonably believes the person has a weapon or is attempting to gain access to one and it is reasonable to believe the person intends to use it against the officer or a third person; 2) the person is capable of causing death or serious bodily injury without a weapon and it is reasonable to believe the person intends to do so; or 3) a person is armed with a weapon but is not at that instant pointing the weapon at the officer or a third person, but is carrying the weapon and is running for cover, or toward a crowd, or has the opportunity to take someone hostage. The duration of imminent danger is context specific and is dependent on the totality of the circumstances in each situation and is not the same in all situations.

19  The *Post* data are not sufficient to analyze negligence.

20  The following court decisions that have ruled police officers are not required to select the least intrusive force option: *United States v. Sokolow*, 490 U.S. 1 (1989); *Roy v. Lewiston*, 42 F.3d 691 (1st Cir. 1994); *Salim v. Proulx*, 93 F.3d 86 (2nd Cir. 1996); *Elliott v. Leavitt*, 99 F.3d 640 (4th Cir. 1996); *Collins v. Nagle*, 892 F.2d 489 (6th Cir. 1989); *Tauke v. Stine*, 120 F.3d 1363 (8th Cir. 1997); *Schulz v. Long*, 44 F.3d 643 (8th Cir. 1995); *Scott v. Henrich*, 39 F.3d 912 (9th Cir. 1994); *Warren v. Las Vegas*, 111 F.3d 139 (9th Cir. 1997); *Wilson v. Meeks*, 52 F.3d 1547 (10th Cir. 1995); *Menual v. Atlanta*, 25 F.3d 990 (11th Cir. 1994); *Medina v. Cram*, 252 F.3d 1124 (10th Cir. 2001) (cited in Petrowski, 2002, p. 30, note #28).

21  See N.J.S.A. 2C:29–2 as one example: "It is not a defense to a prosecution under this subsection that the law enforcement officer was acting unlawfully in making the arrest, provided he was acting under color of his official authority and provided the law enforcement officer announces his intention to arrest prior to the resistance."

# 3 National Police Use of Force Data

## Methodology

When traditional or official data sources are unavailable to study a given phenomenon, scholars have used open-source data as an alternative, such as studies involving political and ideological violence (LaFree & Dugan, 2007) and various forms of terrorism (Freilich et al., 2014; Smith & Damphousse, 2007). Official data sources for studying police shooting fatalities are either incomplete or do not exist (Alpert, 2016; Shane, 2016); therefore, we rely on open-source data from the *Washington Post*. The data are publicly available and were obtained freely from the *Washington Post* "Fatal Force Database" of 2015–2016.[1] The *Post* data project is intended to collect publicly available reports on police use of force incidents that result in death from news reports, law enforcement websites, social media, and independent databases such as Killed by Police and Fatal Encounters to get a better sense of the number of police fatalities in the United States.

The strength of data is that it does not capture fatalities involving people in police custody, federal sworn officers, shootings by off-duty officers, corrections officers, or non-shooting deaths, which are reflected in other similar sources.[2] By restricting the analysis to only those fatalities involving on-duty officers who killed someone with a firearm, the results more accurately reflect police officers who are working in an official capacity and who are acting under color of authority. Another strength is that when compared to federal or state sources, open sources such as the *Post* have been shown to capture between 30% and 45% more cases, which ensures more reliable estimates and more data to answer important questions (Williams, Bowman & Jung, 2016; also see Wiersema, Loftin & McDowall, 2000).

Police fatalities are a form of homicide and homicide studies relying on open-source data have been shown to be as effective as official data in identifying individual- and situational-level characteristics (Gruenewald, 2012, 2013; Parkin & Gruenwald, 2017; also see Fox & Levin, 2005; Quinet, 2011). More specifically, validating media-driven and crowdsourced police shooting data on the incidence of officer-involved fatalities has been shown to be generally consistent across various open-source data sets including the *Washington Post* (Ozkan, Worrall & Zettler, 2017).

The database is rolling, which means that it is updated periodically as police shootings occur; the data for this study are from January 2, 2015 to December 29, 2016; these are the same data that were used for two other studies involving use of force and were used in this study to maintain consistency (Shane, 2016; Shane, Lawton & Swenson, 2017). The unit of analysis is the shooting incident. Only fatalities classified by the *Post* as unarmed are used for this study.[3]

News articles for each fatality were collected via four Internet search engines; Bing, Yahoo, and Google are three leading search engines,[4] and Dogpile is a meta search engine that sends requests to several other search engines and/or databases simultaneously and aggregates the results into a single return. The articles were reviewed to identify the imminent threat facing the officer or the public when force was used. An imminent threat is defined as threatened actions or outcomes that may occur during an encounter absent action by a law enforcement officer. "Imminency," as a standard to meet before using force, suggests the threatened harm does not necessarily have to be instantaneous; for example, an imminent threat may exist even if a subject is not at that instant pointing a weapon at the officer, but is carrying a weapon and running for cover, attempting to take a hostage, or is unarmed and attacking the officer.[5] To minimize subjective inaccuracies, a data collection protocol was used to extract the data based on the concepts shown in table 3.1.

Twenty cases were removed from the analysis because the news articles did not disclose enough information to determine whether the officer or the public was facing an imminent threat, and so the nature of the encounter was undetermined;[6] the analysis includes only complete cases and no effort was made to impute or otherwise substitute data with hypothetical values. The final sample size is 112, and

*Table 3.1* Conceptual Definitions for the Types of Threats Facing a Police Officer

| Confrontation Type | Conceptual Definition |
| --- | --- |
| **Physical assault** | Occurs when an offender is: 1) attempting to drown an officer; 2) attempting to disarm an officer; 3) attempting to throw an officer from an elevated position (balcony, rooftop, bridge, stairs, etc.; 4) attempting to push an officer into vehicular traffic; 5) physically choking an officer; 6) placing an officer in a headlock; 7) pushing the officer to ground and mounting the officer; 8) physically striking the officer using hands, feet, or teeth, or wrestling or struggling with the officer; 9) physically striking an officer's head against a surface (ground, wall); or 10) disarming an officer or another officer of a piece of equipment (gun, radio, baton, TASER, handcuffs, other equipment). |
| **Perceptual threat of an imminent assault** | Occurs when an offender communicates by a gesture that simulates an attack, although a physical assault does not occur. Physical gestures that simulate an attack include when an offender is: 1) reaching into his/her waistband, pockets, or behind their back, or otherwise concealing their hands from the officer's view during the course of committing a crime or flight therefrom; 2) reaching under the car seat or into the car during the course of committing a crime or flight therefrom; 3) issuing verbal threats; 4); advancing or charging at the officer; 5) assuming a shooting or fighting stance (with no handheld objects); 6) simulating a shooting stance with an object other than a weapon (vaping device, metal pen, cell phone); or 7) engaging in unspecified threatening or aggressive movements. |
| **Attempting to arm self with weapon** | Occurs when the offender tries to gain control of a physical weapon (e.g., gun, knife, club, stick, etc.) other than a weapon carried by the officer. |
| **Escaping or eluding officers using a vehicle and recklessly endangering the public or other officers after being ordered to stop** | Occurs when the offender is using a vehicle and refuses to cease and desist from threatening behavior, but is not directly attacking anyone with the vehicle. |
| **Accidental shooting** | Occurs when an officer deliberately pulls the trigger of his or her firearm, but transfers intent and shoots another person as in a crossfire situation or homicide by misadventure. |
| **Unintentional discharge** | Occurs when discharging the officer's firearm at a time not intended by the officer, such as from a mechanical malfunction, or during dry-fire practice or a demonstration. |

although a smaller sample decreases power, the advantage is that it leads to unbiased parameter estimates (Little & Rubin, 1987). Early adulthood citizens, those believed to be in greatest contact with police, were measured as those between 20 and 39, which was conceptualized by Erikson's (1963, 1980) psychosocial development scale and is consistent with similar studies involving young adults (Whitbourne et al., 1992). The research questions are:

1   During the observation period, what is the yearly incidence of unarmed fatal police shootings during certain encounters?
2   Which type of unarmed encounter presents the greatest risk?
3   What proportion of officers was indicted for shooting an unarmed citizen?
4   What type of unarmed encounter is likely to result in an indictment?
5   Do nonwhites exhibit more imminent threatening behavior than whites?

**Power Analysis**

Statistical power is the probability of detecting a meaningful difference, or effect, if one actually exists (Weisburd, Petrosino & Mason, 1993, p. 340). To test the data, the primary analytic techniques are a chi-square test of independence and analysis of variance (ANOVA). Power was assessed using 2018 Statistical Decision Tree software (Table 3.2).[7] Tests for normality using histograms show the data is relatively normally distributed; both the chi-square test of independence and ANOVA are not heavily dependent on the normality assumptions (Norusis, 2010, p. 309). The power analysis suggests that this research is likely to detect significant effects since the sample is 112 cases. Although power estimates vary a bit across statistical tests, this study's design allows for high statistical power if effects are large or moderate.

*Table 3.2* Power Analysis

| Statistical Test | Sample Size | Power | D.F | Groups | Effect size | p |
|---|---|---|---|---|---|---|
| Chi-Square | 49.060 | 0.8 | 1 | — | 0.4 | 0.05 |
| ANOVA | 18.040 | 0.8 | — | 4 | 0.4 | 0.05 |

# Notes

1 Retrieved on June 20, 2017 from www.washingtonpost.com/graphics/national/ police-shootings/.
2 See both retrieved on January 20, 2017 from Killed by Police (www. http://killed-bypolice.net/) and Fatal Encounters (www.fatalencounters.org/).
3 After review, nine cases were removed from the analysis since the citizen was not unarmed, but was actually armed during the encounter: 1) Lavall Hall, Miami Gardens, FL, 2/15/2015, Metal-tipped broomstick; 2) Bobby Gross, Washington, DC, 3/12/2015, Tree branch; 3) Jamison Childress, Sumas, WA, 3/19/2015, Bear spray; 4) Alfredo Rias-Torres, Arlington, VA, 5/19/2015, Metal pole; 5) Darren Billy Wilson, White, GA, 7/21/2015, Tree branch; 6) Vernell Bing, Jacksonville, FL, 5/22/2016, Vehicle; 7) John Paul Quintero, Wichita, KS, 1/3/2015, Knife; 8) Antonio Zambrano-Montes, Pasco, WA, 2/10/2015, Rocks; and 9) Michael Eugene Wilson, Jr., Hallandale Beach, FL, 5/22/2016, Vehicle.
4 Retrieved on July 10, 2017 from https://searchenginewatch.com/2016/08/08/ what-are-the-top-10-most-popular-search-engines/.
5 See *Montoute v. Carr*, 114 F.3d 181 (11th Cir. 1997). Police responded to a report of shots fired at a party. Upon arrival, a police officer heard a gunshot and then encountered Montoute carrying a sawed-off shotgun. Two officers repeatedly ordered Montoute to drop the shotgun. He refused and continued approaching. He then passed the officers and took off running. One officer shot Montoute in the buttock and he subsequently filed a 1983 civil action. The court held: "In view of all of the facts, we cannot say that an officer in those volatile circumstances could not reasonably have believed that Montoute might wheel around and fire his shotgun again, or might take cover behind a parked automobile or the side of a building and shoot at the officers or others. Indeed, if the officers had allowed Montoute to take cover, or perhaps circle back around to the crowd, he could have posed even more danger than when he had presented a clear target as he approached them." The court ruled in favor of the officer.
6 1) Michael Ireland, 2/17/2015, Springfield, MO; 2) Jeremy Lett, 2/04/2015, Tallahassee, FL; 3) Daniel Kevin Harris, 8/18/2016, Charlotte, NC; 4) Jose Raul Cruz, 3/13/2016, Addison, TX; 5) Richard Jacquez, 8/17/2015, San Jose, CA; 6) Matthew Dobbins, 10/02/2015, Amarillo, TX; 7) Livonia Riggins, 10/2/2015, Tampa, FL; 8) Terence Crutcher, 9/16/2016, Tulsa, OK; 9) Deravis Caine Rogers, 6/22/2016, Atlanta, GA; 10) Brandon Stanley, 3/4/2016, East Berstadt, KY; 11) Samuel Dubose, 7/19/2015, Mt. Auburn, OH; 12) Kris Jackson, 6/15/2015, South Lake Tahoe, CA; 13) Brendon Glenn, 5/5/2015, Venice, CA; 14) Walter Scott, 4/4/2015, North Charleston, SC; 15) Sergio Alexander Navas, 3/5/2015, Burbank, CA; 16) Derek Cruice, 3/4/2015, Deltona, FL; 17) Ernesto Javier Canepa Diaz, 2/27/2015, Santa Ana, CA; 18) Daniel Elrod, 2/23/2015, Omaha, NE; 19) Ruben Villalpando, 2/20/2015, Euless, TX; and 20) Richard Carlin, 2/13/2015, Reading, PA.
7 Retrieved on January 20, 2018 from www.anzmtg.org/stats/PowerCalculator/ PowerChiSquare. GPower 3.1 (2014) software suggests a sample size of 76 for ANOVA, which is below the sample size of 112 in this study.

# 4    Data Analysis and Results

## Descriptive Statistics

Table 4.1 shows the descriptive statistics in the study. The unarmed fatal encounters were grouped into five categories: 1) physical assaults (47.3%); 2) perceptual threat of an imminent assault (35.7%); 3) accidental shootings/unintentional discharge (11.6%); 4) escaping or eluding while endangering the public (3.6%); and 5) attempting to arm self with a weapon (1.8%). The number of unarmed fatalities between 2015 (*n*=73) and 2016 (*n*=39) declined 46.6%. Citizens are mostly male (94.6%) and White (40.2%), followed closely by Blacks (38.4%). Early adulthood citizens (age 20–39), those believed to be in greatest contact with the police (see Eith & Durose, 2011), are the largest group of citizens (64.0%). The south (37.5%) and west (34.8%) are the leading regions[1] of the country for unarmed fatal encounters; the northeast is well below the other regions (5.4%). Most police officers were not indicted (92.9%). As for a citizen's flight status, most citizens were not fleeing when they were shot (57.7%), which indicates they were at least standing their ground against the officer or were not under control. This is followed by citizens who were fleeing in a vehicle after being ordered to stop (17.1%), which presents a public safety threat.

Eighty-three percent of fatalities involving unarmed citizens were either through physical assaults (47.3%) or perceptual threats of an imminent assault (35.7%). Various types of physical assaults, which are clearly an attack upon an officer, dominate the justification for shooting an unarmed citizen. Personal weapons, the most readily available weapon, comprise the majority of assaults (60.4%), which is consistent with FBI LEOKA data. This is followed by disarming

*Table 4.1* Descriptive Statistics in the Study (*n* = 112)

| Variable | n | % of Total | % of Group |
|---|---|---|---|
| *Categories of Unarmed Fatal Encounters* | | | |
| **Physical Assault** | **53** | **47.3** | **100.0** |
| Personal weapons; wrestled or struggled with the officer | 32 | 28.6 | 60.4 |
| Attempted to disarm officer | 11 | 9.8 | 20.8 |
| Disarmed the officer or other officer (gun, radio, baton, TASER, handcuffs, other equipment) | 4 | 3.6 | 7.5 |
| Attempted to drown officer | 3 | 2.7 | 5.7 |
| Attempted to throw officer from an elevated position (balcony, rooftop, bridge, stairs, etc.) | 1 | 0.9 | 1.9 |
| Choked the officer | 1 | 0.9 | 1.9 |
| Pushed the officer to the ground and mounted the officer | 1 | 0.9 | 1.9 |
| **Perceptual Threat of an Imminent Assault** | **40** | **35.7** | **100.0** |
| Advancing/charging toward the officer | 14 | 12.5 | 35.0 |
| Hands in pockets, waistband, or behind back, or otherwise concealed from officer during a crime or flight therefrom | 11 | 9.8 | 27.5 |
| Shooting or fighting stance (empty handed) | 6 | 5.4 | 15.0 |
| Simulating shooting stance/gesturing as if armed with object other than a real weapon (vaping device, cell phone, metal pen) | 5 | 4.5 | 12.5 |
| Unspecified threatening/aggressive movement[1] | 3 | 2.7 | 7.5 |
| Reaching under car seat or inside car during course of committing a crime or flight therefrom | 1 | 0.9 | 2.5 |
| **Accidental Shooting/Unintentional Discharge** | **13** | **11.6** | **100.0** |
| Accidental shooting (cross fire situation; homicide by misadventure) | 11 | 9.8 | 84.6 |
| Unintentional discharge | 2 | 1.8 | 15.4 |
| **Escaping or Eluding and Endangering the Public After Being Ordered to Stop** | **4** | **3.6** | **100.0** |
| Escaping or eluding officers using a vehicle while recklessly endangering the public or other officers | 4 | 3.6 | 30.8 |
| **Attempting to Arm Self with Weapon** | **2** | **1.8** | **100.0** |
| Attempting to arm self with a weapon | 2 | 1.8 | 15.4 |
| **Year** | **112** | **100.0** | — |
| 2015 | 73 | 65.2 | — |
| 2016 | 39 | 34.8 | — |
| **Citizen's Sex** | **112** | **100.0** | — |
| Male | 106 | 94.6 | — |
| Female | 6 | 5.4 | — |
| **Citizen's Race** | **112** | **100.0** | — |
| White | 45 | 40.2 | — |
| Black | 43 | 38.4 | — |
| Hispanic | 18 | 16.1 | — |

| Variable | n | % of Total | % of Group |
|---|---|---|---|
| *Categories of Unarmed Fatal Encounters* | | | |
| Other | 4 | 3.6 | — |
| Native American | 2 | 1.8 | — |
| **Early Adulthood Citizens** | **111** | **100.0** | — |
| 20–39 | 71 | 64.0 | — |
| All Others | 40 | 36.0 | — |
| **Region** | **112** | **100.0** | — |
| South | 42 | 37.5 | — |
| West | 39 | 34.8 | — |
| Midwest | 25 | 22.3 | — |
| Northeast | 6 | 5.4 | — |
| **Officer Indicted?** | **112** | **100.0** | — |
| Not Indicted | 104 | 92.9 | — |
| Indicted | 8 | 7.1 | — |
| **Citizen's Flight Status** | **111** | **100.0** | — |
| Not Fleeing | 64 | 57.7 | — |
| By Car | 19 | 17.1 | — |
| By Foot | 24 | 21.6 | — |
| Other Means | 4 | 3.6 | — |

1 The articles did not reveal the type of threatening gesture, they only referenced vague language that the citizen "indicated" they had a weapon or were acting "aggressively" toward the officer without articulating more details.

and attempting to disarm an officer (28.3%). Perceptual threats of an imminent assault are physical movements or verbal actions that are communicated through a citizen's gesturing that simulate or precede an attack, although a physical assault does not actually occur because it may have been preempted by the officer's reaction, or other circumstance. These types of threats often occur as a cluster of body movements, words, and facial expressions that signal imminent danger and may occur suddenly.[2] Advancing or charging toward the officer is a large, aggressive movement of the entire body and is the leading perceptual threat (35.0%) whose primary intent is to incite aggression. This is followed closely by a citizen who is concealing their hands from the officer's view (27.5%), which forecasts the citizen is about to launch an attack.[3] Many citizens also engaged in mock attacks, symbolic actions that mimic a real attack. In 27.5% of the encounters, citizens either assumed a mock shooting or fighting stance while empty handed (15.0%) or simulated a shooting stance as if they were armed with a weapon (12.5%).

Two types of unarmed fatalities emerged that may carry a degree of negligence. The accidental shooting and the unintentional discharge account for 11.6% of fatalities. An accidental shooting is when an officer deliberately pulls the trigger of his or her firearm, but transfers intent and shoots another person as in a crossfire situation or homicide by misadventure (9.8%). An unintentional discharge is when the officer's firearm is discharged at a time not intended by the officer, such as from a mechanical malfunction, or during dry-fire practice or a demonstration (1.8%).

One of the least common types of threat is when a citizen is escaping or eluding officers using a vehicle and recklessly endangers the public or other officers after being ordered to stop (3.6%). When the citizen is using a vehicle and refuses to cease and desist from threatening behavior (e.g., initiating a motor vehicle pursuit), but does not directly attack anyone with the vehicle, the situation may amount to a deadly force encounter. Lastly, the least prevalent type of encounter is when a citizen is attempting to arm themselves with a weapon (1.8%) (other than attempting to disarm the officer), which could have been any type of weapon, not necessarily a knife or a gun.

## Answering the Research Questions

### *Yearly Incidence of Unarmed Fatal Encounters*

Establishing incidence is important so there is some sense of the scope of the problem. Incidence is limited to the number of new cases during a specified time period, in this analysis 2015 and 2016. Incidence is measured as the proportion of unarmed threats during a police-citizen encounter that results in a fatality. Between 2015 ($n$=73) and 2016 ($n$=39), there were 112 fatalities (5.7% of all fatal shootings during the period)[4] involving unarmed citizens according to the *Post* data. The U.S. Bureau of Justice Statistics (BJS) estimates that in 2008 the number of police-citizen contacts was 40,015,000 (Eith & Durose, 2011, Table 4.1, p. 2).[5] Recognizing that all types of police-citizen contacts do not have equal chance of resulting in a fatality (such as during assistance or service contacts, which are not typically high risk), we estimate the incidence of fatal shootings during unarmed but threating encounters only (upper panel of Table 4.2), which is a subset of the BJS data that reflect risky situations; the denominator is the

*Table 4.2* Incidence of Unarmed Threats (*n* = 112)

| Year | Threat Group | n | % | Yearly Incidence Proportion (Risk) |
|------|-------------|---|---|-----------------------------------|
| **2015** | Physical Assault | 38 | 52.1 | 0.0001249 |
| | Perceptual Threat | 21 | 28.8 | 0.0000690 |
| | Accidental/Unintentional Discharge | 10 | 13.7 | 0.0000329 |
| | Attempting to Arm Self with Weapon | 2 | 2.7 | 0.0000066 |
| | Escaping or Eluding and Endangering the Public | 2 | 2.7 | 0.0000047 |
| | **Total** | **73** | **100.0** | |
| **2016** | Physical Assault | 15 | 38.5 | 0.0000493 |
| | Perceptual Threat | 19 | 48.7 | 0.0000624 |
| | Accidental/Unintentional Discharge | 3 | 7.7 | 0.0000099 |
| | Escaping or Eluding and Endangering the Public | 2 | 5.1 | 0.0000066 |
| | **Total** | **39** | **100.0** | |

Incidence of Unarmed Threats Resulting in Indictment (*n* = 8)

| Year | Threat Group | n | % | Yearly Incidence Proportion (Risk) |
|------|-------------|---|---|-----------------------------------|
| **2015** | Physical Assault | 1 | 14.3 | 0.0000033 |
| | Perceptual Threat | 3 | 42.9 | 0.0000099 |
| | Accidental/Unintentional Discharge | 3 | 42.9 | 0.0000099 |
| | **Total** | **7** | **100.0** | |
| **2016** | Perceptual Threat | 1 | 28.8 | 0.0000033 |
| | **Total** | **1** | **100.0** | |

sum of police-contacts in 2008 (*n*=30,427,008) during a traffic stop (*n*=17,663,000), as a passenger during a traffic stop (*n*=1,146,000), after a resident reported a crime/problem to police (*n*=8,345,000), while police were investigating a crime (*n*=2,257,000), and when police suspected a resident of wrongdoing (*n*=1,014,000).

As Johnson (2016, p. 3) notes, compared to other unnatural causes of death identified by the U.S. Centers for Disease Control in 2015 including criminal homicide (*n*=16,121), traffic accidents (*n*=33,804), and medical errors (*n*=251,454), the risk of a police-citizen encounter ending in a shooting fatality is extremely low (*n*=112) and can hardly be described as a crisis or an epidemic, as some observers have suggested (see Calacal, 2017). With the exception of escaping or eluding, all categories of unarmed threats decreased in 2016, or remained the same from 2015. If we use indictments resulting from fatal shootings as a measure of unjustified police shootings, then the incidence of unlawful police behavior is even lower (lower panel of Table 4.2).

### Types of Unarmed Encounters That Present the Greatest Risk

An important principle of risk analysis is that outcomes are highly concentrated among particular situations. This implies that focusing efforts where police shooting fatalities are concentrated may yield the greatest preventive benefits. To examine risk further, Pareto analysis (also known as the 80/20 rule, Clarke & Eck, 2005, pp. 48–49) was applied to the types of encounters an officer is likely to face (Table 4.3, Figure 4.1), which helps answer the second research

*Table 4.3* Pareto Analysis of Unarmed Fatal Encounters ($n = 112$)

| Categories of Unarmed Fatal Encounters | Fatalities (n) | Cumulative Fatalities (n) | % of Fatalities | Cumulative % of Fatalities | Cumulative % of Unarmed Encounters |
|---|---|---|---|---|---|
| 1. Personal weapons; wrestled or struggled with the officer | 32 | 32 | 28.6 | 28.6 | 5.9 |
| 2. Advancing/charging toward the officer | 14 | 46 | 12.5 | 41.1 | 11.8 |
| 3. Attempted to disarm officer | 11 | 57 | 9.8 | 50.9 | 17.6 |
| 4. Hands in pockets, waistband, or behind back, or otherwise concealed from officer during crime or flight therefrom | 11 | 68 | 9.8 | 60.7 | 23.5 |
| 5. Accidental shooting (crossfire) | 11 | 79 | 9.8 | 70.5 | 29.4 |
| 6. Shooting or fighting stance (empty handed) | 6 | 85 | 5.4 | 75.9 | 35.3 |
| 7. Simulating shooting stance/gesturing as if armed with object other than a weapon (vaping device, cell phone, metal pen) | 5 | 90 | 4.5 | 80.4 | 41.2 |

| Categories of Unarmed Fatal Encounters | Fatalities (n) | Cumulative Fatalities (n) | % of Fatalities | Cumulative % of Fatalities | Cumulative % of Unarmed Encounters |
|---|---|---|---|---|---|
| 8. Escaping or eluding officers using a vehicle and recklessly endangering the public or other officers | 4 | 94 | 3.6 | 83.9 | 47.1 |
| 9. Disarmed the officer or other officer (gun, radio, baton, TASER, handcuffs, other equipment) | 4 | 98 | 3.6 | 87.5 | 52.9 |
| 10. Attempted to drown officer | 3 | 101 | 2.7 | 90.2 | 58.8 |
| 11. Unspecified threatening/ aggressive movement | 3 | 104 | 2.7 | 92.9 | 64.7 |
| 12. Attempting to arm self with a weapon | 2 | 106 | 1.8 | 94.6 | 70.6 |
| 13. Accidental shooting/ unintentional discharge | 2 | 108 | 1.8 | 96.4 | 76.5 |
| 14. Attempted to throw officer from an elevated position (balcony, rooftop, bridge, stairs, etc.) | 1 | 109 | 0.9 | 97.3 | 82.4 |
| 15. Physically choked the officer | 1 | 110 | 0.9 | 98.2 | 88.2 |
| 16. Pushed the officer to the ground and mounted the officer | 1 | 111 | 0.9 | 99.1 | 94.1 |
| 17. Reaching under car seat or inside car during course of committing a crime or flight therefrom | 1 | 112 | 0.9 | 100.0 | 100.0 |
| Total | 112 | – | 100.0% | – | – |

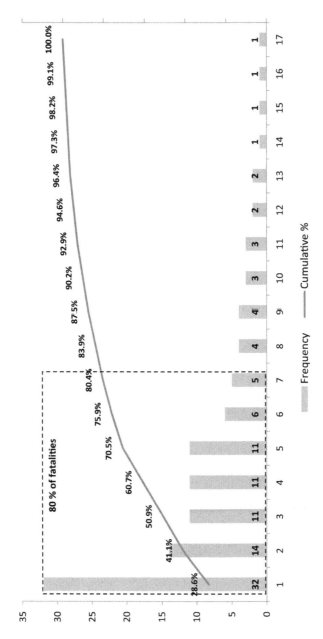

*Figure 4.1* Pareto Analysis of Unarmed Encounters ($n = 112$) with 30% Region

question: *Which threats present the greatest risk to a police officer or the public?* Pareto analysis is a decision-making technique used to express that a limited number of phenomena (e.g., threats to the officer or the public) produce the majority of outcomes (e.g., police shooting fatalities involving unarmed citizens). In the present context, Pareto helps focus training and policy efforts on the encounters that offer the greatest potential for improvement by comparing their relative magnitude and frequency in descending order. There are 17 types of unarmed encounters, where about one-quarter (23.5%) of the encounters accounts for approximately two-thirds (60.7%) of the fatalities. In theory, focusing preventive action through policy development, decision-making, tactical training, and situational awareness on these five types of encounters, rather than on all 17 types, could be an efficient strategy for reducing police fatalities involving unarmed citizens nationwide.

### Unarmed Fatalities That Result In Indictments

An important and persistent social question about police shootings involving unarmed citizens is how often these encounters end with an indictment and what type of unarmed encounter generates the most indictments (Table 4.4). The overwhelming proportion of fatalities

*Table 4.4* Type of Unarmed Fatal Encounter Resulting in an Indictment

| Type of Unarmed Encounter | | Officer Indicted? | | |
|---|---|---|---|---|
| | | No | Yes | Total |
| Physical Assault | n | 52 | 1 | 53 |
| | % | 46.4 | 0.9 | 47.3 |
| Perceptual Threat of an Imminent Assault | n | 36 | 4 | 40 |
| | % | 32.1 | 3.6 | 35.7 |
| Accidental Shooting/Unintentional Discharge | n | 10 | 3 | 13 |
| | % | 8.9 | 2.7 | 11.6 |
| Attempting to Arm Self with Weapon | n | 2 | 0 | 2 |
| | % | 1.8 | 0.0 | 1.8 |
| Escaping or Eluding and Endangering the Public | n | 4 | 0 | 4 |
| | % | 3.6 | 0.0 | 3.6 |
| **Total** | n | **104** | **8** | **112** |
| | % | **92.9** | **7.1** | **100.0** |

did not end in an indictment (92.9%), and one fatality ended in a federal indictment for a civil rights violation. Only one case where an officer faced a physical assault resulted in an indictment (0.9%).[6] Perceptual threats of an impending assault (3.6%) and accidental shooting/unintentional discharge (2.7%) resulted in the most indictments. A chi-square test of independence suggests that although there is no relationship between the type of unarmed encounter and whether or not the officer was indicted ($\chi^2(4) =8.138$, $p=.087$; $V=.270$),[7] indictments for accidental shooting/unintentional discharge and perceptual threats were slightly higher than expected. However, this is somewhat expected given that perceptual threats of an impending assault must be sufficiently articulated and coupled with a manifest threat to ensure an encounter is more than just the product of an officer's subjective fear; restated, fear alone is not sufficient to justify deadly force. This finding is also expected since fatalities resulting from accidental shootings/unintentional discharge may carry a degree of negligence in how the officer handled the situation.[8]

Other important questions about the relationship between criminal indictments and characteristics of the encounter such as age, race, sex,[9] flight status, and region of the country also exist. These are just some of the expectations society is entitled to have answered about shootings involving unarmed citizens. Table 4.5 answers some of these questions, albeit in limited form given the dearth of data.[10] There is no relationship between any of the encounters and whether the fatality resulted in an indictment based on age, race, and flight status in a

*Table 4.5* Chi-Square Analysis Comparing Fatal Encounters Resulting in Indictment

| Variables | Question | Finding | N | $\chi^2$ | P[1] | V |
|---|---|---|---|---|---|---|
| Age (20–39; others) | Are unarmed encounters more likely to end in indictment with young-adult citizens? | No | 111 | 2.619 | 0.134 | 0.154 |
| Race (white; nonwhite) | Are unarmed encounters more likely to end in indictment with nonwhite citizens? | No | 112 | 0.346 | 0.712 | 0.056 |
| Flight Status (fleeing; not fleeing) | Are unarmed encounters more likely to end in indictment when a citizen is fleeing? | No | 107 | 0.026 | 1.000 | 0.016 |

1 Fisher's Exact Test due to low expected cell counts less than 5.

bivariate model. Region of the country was analyzed using analysis of variance (ANOVA) (indicted=1). The Northeast had the highest mean score for indictments (0.17), followed by the South (0.09), West (0.05), and the Midwest (0.04), but there is no significant difference between regions ($F(3, 108)=.585, p=.626$).

These findings suggest that there are likely additional factors driving the decision to indict an officer for fatally shooting an unarmed citizen; a prosecutor's decision is predicated on the lack of probable cause based on the totality of the circumstances, which subsumes necessity, proportionality, and imminence instead of explanations such as age, race, or sex. If police officers properly apply their training and legal authority during use of force situations, then fatalities are dependent on the type of threat they encounter, not extra-legal factors such as age, sex, and race (*Graham v. Connor*, 1989; *Tennessee v. Garner*, 1985). To determine whether the police are fatally shooting people in an unjustified manner, it is necessary to account for the offender's actions during the encounter, such as those described in Table 4.1; the offender's actions shown in Table 4.1 are not available through the *Post* data.

A similar persistent question often mentioned by scholars and the public is not whether an officer can be found justified when they are involved in a fatality with an unarmed offender based on articulable facts; the problem is whether these articulable facts appear more often when an incident involves a nonwhite person. Table 4.6 shows the

*Table 4.6* Distribution of Described Threats Based on Decedent's Race ($n = 112$)

| Threat Group | | Decedent's Race | | Total |
| --- | --- | --- | --- | --- |
| | | Nonwhite | White | |
| Physical Assault; Perceptual Threat of an Imminent Assault (=1) | $n$ | 57 | 36 | 93 |
| All Other Threats (Accidental Shooting/ Unintentional Discharge; Escaping or Eluding and Endangering the Public After Being Ordered to Stop; Attempting to Arm Self with Weapon) (=0) | $n$ | 10 | 9 | 19 |
| **Total** | $n$ | 67 | 45 | 112 |
| | % | 59.8 | 40.2 | 100.0 |

$X^2(1) =.492, p=.483$

distribution of observed threats based on the decedent's race. The data show that media accounts tend to describe imminent threating behavior from nonwhites more so than from whites. The threat group data were collapsed[11] into two categories (physical assaults and perceptual threats=1 and all other threats=0) and showed no statistically significant difference. This is consistent with similar research on this topic using the same data (Shane, 2016; Shane, Lawton & Swenson, 2017). Although social factors are at the forefront of the national debate about police use of force, an encounter that results in death is likely more complex than a few sociodemographic characteristics (e.g., MacDonald, 2016), particularly race, which is usually the impetus for a riot.

## Notes

1  U.S. regions according to the FBI Uniform Crime Report: *Northeast*: ME, NH, VT, MA, CT, RI, NY, PA, NJ; *South*: TX, OK, AR, LA, AL, GA, KY, TN, WV, VA, DE, MD, DC, NC, SC, FL, MS; *Midwest*: ND, SD, NB, KS, MN, IA, MO, MI, WI, IL, IN, OH; *West*: WA, OR, CA, HI, AK, ID, NV, MT, WY, CO, AZ, UT, NM.

2  Words, facial expressions, and hand gestures are important indicators of aggression or intent, but not all of them were available from the news articles.

3  Police officers are customarily trained to observe a person's hands during an interaction since the hands are nearly always used to strike (see, as one example, New Jersey Police Training Commission, Patrol Techniques, Performance Objective 10.3.13, "the trainee will identify the reasons for always having a suspect's hands in plain view," p. 167).

4  There were 1,948 fatal shootings for 2015 and 2016 in the *Post* dataset.

5  This is the latest available data for police-public contacts.

6  Brandon Jones, Cleveland, OH, 3/19/2015.

7  Using the lower alpha level of 0.10 suggests there are statistically significant differences for accidental shooting/unintentional discharge and perceptual threats. Although lowering the alpha level is not consistent with statistical convention, indictments for these categories of unarmed encounters are slightly higher than expected. Compared to physical assaults, the result is consistent with what might be reasonable given the totality of the circumstances when an encounter ends in a fatality and is not supported by the evidence.

8  Neither the *Post* data nor the news articles enable a deeper analysis of the situational characteristics of the accidental shooting/unintentional discharge category.

9  Sex cannot be computed because there is no variability; there are no cases involving female fatality victims that resulted in indictment in which to calculate comparisons. Similarly, the *Post*'s variable "signs of mental illness" was purposely excluded from analysis since mental illness is a very complex condition that is not defined by the *Post*'s methodology. Also, there is no data source upon which

to calculate base rates so deriving reliable estimates was not possible. Given the complexity of the phenomenon, we felt it best to avoid drawing unreliable conclusions from incomplete data.

10  The available data from the *Post* are limited and do not enable a robust analysis beyond bivariate relationships (see Shane, 2016 for similar limitations of the *Post*'s data).

11  Given the small sample, collapsing the data was required to avoid low cell counts during the chi-square crosstab analysis. Although this leads to some loss of fidelity, the parameter estimates are more reliable.

# 5   Discussion of the Findings and Policy Implications

This study sought to examine more closely the nature of the encounter when a fatality occurred involving the police and an unarmed citizen and the patterns that emerged. The federal statutory law and case law standards that govern police use of force do not establish an absolute prohibition against using deadly force toward an unarmed citizen, so it's critical to know just what type of threat an officer was facing that provided probable cause to use deadly force. The law requires a police officer must act reasonably when they apply force and being unarmed is but one factor the courts will consider when assessing the threat an officer was facing. The *Post*'s unarmed classification is, at best, a technicality—insofar as citizens may not physically possess a weapon at the moment they were killed—that is not informed by law or contemporary police practices. To the layperson, an unarmed citizen is defenseless against an armed police officer, but a closer look reveals that unarmed status—without further qualification—is fraught with misconceptions when taking into account the threat that prompted the shooting.

Although most people are influenced by emotions to a certain degree, the influence emotion exerts is fallacious when it becomes the basis for deciding the soundness of an argument. While it may be reasonable to show empathy toward someone injured or killed during a use of force episode, that display of emotion should not influence judgment as to questions of fact. The word "unarmed" conjures up an image, an attitude, and an emotional appeal more favorable to the decedent than the unadorned facts elicit. When salient information is withheld or omitted, it is easier to persuade onlookers to accept the argument that the shooting is unjustified because the victim was unarmed. The *Post* data do not capture relevant context and leave unarmed status unqualified.

[handwritten: handle situations such as these if their police officers don't have guns.]

[handwritten margin: so then how do other countries]

Presenting only two choices (armed or unarmed) without further qualification may inadvertently create the fallacy of bifurcation. The armed-unarmed dichotomy presents an "either . . . or" proposition, when in reality there is a range of threatening behavior an unarmed individual may pose; simply because the person is unarmed does not mean they are not dangerous or violent. The armed-unarmed classification is not the end of the argument, but rather it is the beginning since the various types of imminent threats an officer confronts are denied by this mutually exclusive choice. By limiting the field to a forced choice (i.e., armed or unarmed), facts and context that are directly relevant to the discussion are omitted, which could certainly influence public opinion as well as a legal outcome (e.g., an indictment). The fact that many people hold favorable or sympathetic emotions associated with an unarmed fatality victim is substituted for actual evidence of the victim's precipitating behavior when the shooting occurred. When the media portrays the victim as unarmed and therefore defenseless (without additional context), the public falls prey to an appeal to popularity as they accept the argument that unarmed means not dangerous because so many others approve of that same argument. Even if the *Post* did not intend to convey the message that being unarmed did not mean nonthreatening, they also did not specify the type of threat the officer faced when force was used.

[handwritten margin: white people / pointed / better]
[handwritten margin: not true]
[handwritten margin: point black]
[handwritten margin: black kid o's thing]

Facts should be used to test the assumptions or principles upon which an argument is based. When facts are revealed they allow onlookers to accept or modify the original assumption (e.g., all unarmed citizens are defenseless and nonthreatening). To start with assumptions (*a priori*) and to use those assumptions as the basis for accepting or rejecting facts is inappropriate; this misconception is often reflected in the statement "I've made up my mind, don't confuse me with the facts." The shooting of Michael Brown in Ferguson, Missouri is an example where widely held assumptions beforehand (i.e., Brown was unarmed and did not pose a threat to the officer) could not be overcome with facts, even facts presented by eyewitnesses during an independent investigation by the U.S. Department of Justice.[1] The assumption that police officer Darren Wilson killed an unarmed,[2] defenseless citizen resulted in several days of rioting, notwithstanding the factual evidence that Brown physically assaulted the officer. The problem in the Brown case is that the pubic granted too much primacy

[handwritten margin: ex Mike Brown thug photo]

[handwritten bottom: what? evidence?]

to the unarmed and defenseless assumption, and when the facts were presented a large segment of the population failed to modify their belief. Maintaining those assumptions created an unwarranted presumption in favor of the operating principle (i.e., unarmed means defenseless and nonthreatening), which was not supported by the relevant evidence; indeed, the objective evidence was rejected by a large proportion of the population as a product of a failed criminal justice system and illegitimate, biased investigators, but likely explains why Officer Wilson was not indicted at the state or federal level.

What also tends to happen is a one-sided assessment when the public fails to consider both sides of the argument. That assessment of the event is often closely aligned with originally held assumptions or principles and may be predicated on rumors, limited information, or lies. Sound decisions generally require both sides of the argument to be presented; then, preference for one argument will prevail on balance. To accept only one side (i.e., unarmed means defenseless and nonthreatening) is to avoid judgment of the balance sought in a rational argument. When relevant information is withheld or omitted, it is difficult if not impossible to reach a sound decision, which is what happens when citizens are labeled by the media as unarmed during a fatal police shooting without further explanation of the characteristics of the encounter.

The risk of dying from a police-citizen encounter is exceptionally low and an unjustified fatality is even lower (see Shane, Lawton & Swenson, 2017, for a discussion of the base rate fallacy, which helps explain why people are fearful or overly concerned about rare events such as dying in a plane crash, or dying from a police shooting; see also Bozeman et al., 2018, for the infrequency of injury resulting from police use of force). The infrequency of police shooting fatalities is not intended to minimize the personal sorrow from such a tragedy, but it is intended to highlight the rarity of such an event, particularly compared to the incidence of other unnatural causes of death such as homicide, traffic accidents, and medical errors. As Johnson (2016) notes in his study of police use of lethal force, although the medical community is responsible for far more unnatural deaths than the police, there is not nearly the same level of public outcry:

> Part of the fear of police use of force deaths stems from the fact we are supposed to trust the police to protect us, not kill us. The same,

however, can be said of doctors and nurses, yet medical errors kill many thousands more Americans annually than do the police.

(p. 3)[3]

*estimates are not factual*

When taken together, the risk of an unjustified fatal police shooting and the misconceptions surrounding shootings of unarmed citizens lead to hasty generalizations that such fatalities have reached epidemic proportions. By our estimates, only eight shootings involving more than 30 million police-citizen contacts were unjustified (as measured by indictments). These few and unrepresentative cases do not establish a pattern or a widespread practice, nor do they prove the assumption that American police officers are biased as some social movements profess; indeed, these eight cases are likely exceptions to any general rule on police use of force that prevails and they more closely align with "a moral panic" resulting from "exaggerated claims and fictitious information" (Shane, 2016, pp. 4–5) than any customary or accepted police practice.

When a use of force occurs, it is the police officer who gets to decide whether or not probable cause exists. That determination is based on the totality of the circumstances in light of the officer's training and experience. As part of their probable cause determination a police officer is expected to conclude "I feared for my life," "I was afraid for the public's safety," "I thought I was going to die," "I was scared to death," or something similar based on their perceptions. However, those conclusions must be supported by specific articulable facts that are observable and can be demonstrated; there must be some objective truth in the real world upon which reasonable police officers would agree before the force will be justified. The facts the officer relied upon are tested against the *Garner* and *Graham* standards for their credibility, and fear alone will not justify using deadly force.

When a police officer is confronted by someone who is armed, probable cause will likely develop quicker given the intrinsic qualities of the weapon. Unless a person is armed with a per se deadly weapon such as a firearm, the determination of deadliness depends on the weapon's use or intended use. How an object is used or intended to be used will determine whether it qualifies as a deadly weapon. Firearms and certain other instruments are per se weapons based on their design. But whether other lawful implements are deadly weapons is dependent on the context. If an implement is used or intended to be used as a weapon, then it is a weapon; if not, it is a potential weapon whose capability remains unrealized. For example, when a person fashions an object that leads a police officer to reasonably believe it is capable of producing death or serious bodily injury, then that person will likely be considered armed for purposes of deadly force analysis. Fake weapons qualify as being "fashioned" for such analysis, including toy guns and pellet guns. Simulating possession will also suffice for such analysis. Whether a simulated weapon exists is determined by the totality of the circumstances, including whether the officer reasonably believes the offender was armed with a weapon to be used against him or her. A person who possesses a pocket knife in their coat pocket is not armed with a deadly weapon when the person never mentions it or uses it against the officer in any way during the encounter; yes, the person is armed, but there is no evidence the knife is a deadly weapon when it is never held by the person nor seen by the officer.

When a person is unarmed, or if a person simulates being armed with a weapon, then something more is generally required to justify an officer's use of force. Ambiguous or equivocal physical gestures that are deliberately combined with threatening words or phrases will likely complete the impression that the person is armed and prepared to use the weapon regardless of whether the person is actually armed. As an example, a police officer will likely have sufficient evidence to use force, even deadly force, when struggling with a person who pretends to reach for something behind their back (or into their waistband, inside their jacket, inside a vehicle, or the vehicle's seat) intending to make the officer believe he or she has a weapon, while simultaneously threatening the officer with their words. If someone declares they have a gun or a knife, and then motions for their waistband or pocket where the weapon is supposedly secreted, then the officer will have sufficient evidence to estimate the person is armed and prepared to use the weapon; these facts will satisfy simulated possession and an actual tangible object is not necessarily required. A rolled-up magazine, a newspaper or a finger inside a person's jacket pocket could be enough to simulate possession, provided the object was fashioned in a manner that leads the officer to believe it was a concealed weapon. A verbal threat from someone such as "I'm gonna kill you, or "I'm gonna shoot you" while simultaneously reaching their hand under their shirt is also likely enough to establish that the person simulated being armed and intended to use a weapon, which will justify using force.

To sustain a criminal conviction under the federal standard (18 U.S.C. § 242), the prosecution must prove the officer acted willfully with the purpose "to deprive a person of a right which has been made specific either by the express terms of the Constitution or laws of the United States or by decisions interpreting them." This is a high standard to meet when an officer is facing a threatening situation in the performance of their duty, and in most instances the prosecutor will not charge the officer because the evidence will not support probable cause for an indictment; when a police officer faces the type of circumstances identified in these encounters, it is easier to understand why only eight cases involving an unarmed citizen resulted in an indictment.

One debatable question that remains is whether a criminal indictment is an objective measure of a justified police shooting fatality. Society turns to the courts and the criminal justice process to resolve interpersonal disputes, criminal transgressions, and to preserve constitutional guarantees. How these disputes and transgressions are resolved is an important political question because the outcomes reflect the relationship between the individual and the State, particularly the dignity of the individual and that of the State (Arnold, 1962). The criminal justice system is heavily laden with discretionary deliberations, which implicates how cases are processed as well as any assessment of fairness and consistency. This research uses indictments as a very limited inquiry into the justifiability of a fatal police shooting as a measure of justice, and these data cannot answer questions of discretion or decision-making.

The *Graham* standard set by the U.S. Supreme Court provides broad principles about when it is permissible for an officer to use force, but the Court defers to individual police agencies to determine how it will incorporate those principles into their policies and training. Restrictive use of force policies can reduce fatal and nonfatal encounters. Policies and training establish how officers will operationalize the legal principles when confronted with a use of force situation, and implementing those principles is subject to labor agreements, culture, technology, and budget. Although there is little disagreement about a police officer's use of force when confronted with someone armed with a gun, the challenge comes to the perceived need for deadly force when a citizen is unarmed. The law grants an officer a degree of leeway in executing their duty even when the threat is not as clear as a raised firearm. Prosecutors and courts are generally mindful of the Supreme Court's command that police "are often forced to make split-second judgments" and should not be subjected to "the 20/20 vision of hindsight" (*Graham v. Connor*, 1989). When a police officer clearly articulates the threat they were facing by citing facts that imply necessity, proportionality, and imminence (such as during a physical assault), prosecutors and courts will likely to defer to the officer's decision. Although *Graham* sets the baseline use of force requirement for policing across the United States, nothing precludes an individual agency from imposing higher standards on its officers when they are permitted to use force.[4]

When a police officer takes enforcement action they are often at a disadvantage. Situations are often tense and ambiguous, which is something the Supreme Court recognized in *Graham*. Situational awareness is essential and officers are trained to judge when a crisis requires the use of force to regain control of a situation. That awareness is predicated on several principles that establish the context, including but not limited to: 1) time (to slow the pace of action through communication); 2) distance (to gain more of it by withdrawing or backing up); 3) cover (making use of impenetrable objects nearby); 4) concealment (making use of penetrable but generally opaque objects that hide the officer's physical presence); 5) communication (to deescalate or coordinate); 6) containment (to keep the situation localized and from spreading); and 7) teamwork (working with other officers and other public safety members to minimize harm, or mitigate its effects). A police officer must interpret these and other situational circumstances quickly and often under very challenging physical and environmental conditions. Because this is difficult and fraught with ambiguity and pressure, courts and prosecutors grant police officers the latitude to be mistaken about the facts presented to them, but demand they be right about the law at the time they applied force (see Sullivan & Gallo, 2017 for one example). This means the facts may be incorrectly interpreted or information may be inaccurate at the moment, but any use of force must be consistent with the law. Nevertheless, this can be a source of community tension since the aftermath is almost always judged from the calm and comfort of an armchair, not from the officer's perspective as the threat materialized.

When a police shooting occurs, society demands officers act reasonably. When they act reasonably, they act legally and justifiably—and while the outcome may offend some people, it is not necessarily criminal. In determining the reasonableness of an officer's force response, the action must be judged through the perspective of a "reasonable officer" (see Terrill, 2009). This test is applied regardless of how compelling the evidence maybe at a later time, without hindsight evaluation, without regard for the officer's underlying intent or motivation and based on established law at the time force was used.

## Limitations

*How can you use the post if not verified?*
*└ Would it not be smart to use FBI work*

The estimates we report here are not exact given the depth of the *Post* data. Capturing the data relies on crowdsourcing and the efforts of journalists who may have missed some fatalities, or may have missed some details in their count. Other sources such as Killed by Police and Fatal Encounters claim to systematically search for fatalities, but there is no method to cross-reference or validate the data before the *Post* releases it to the public. In short, the *Post* data are not verified, audited by an external source, or confirmed. Some jurisdictions may not publicly report police fatalities (e.g., Kyle, 2014); the voluntary nature of reporting and releasing such information means there is a degree of variation in disclosing fatalities to the public. Similarly, there is no federal mandate that police agencies report officer-involved fatalities to any State agency for quality assurance (i.e., error checking) before the data are publicly released. Although publicly reporting police fatalities is an essential function of government accountability, some agencies may not be as attentive as they should be, or may be outright hostile toward the media so they may forgo this accepted routine practice. This lack of uniformity in reporting standards and procedures likely contributes to undercounting (Kyle, 2014; Loftin et al., 2003). Although media accounts of fatalities by police cannot be easily verified by researchers, the data are more comprehensive than current U.S. government sources (Miller et al., 2017; Williams, Bowman & Jung, 2016) and scholars have validated media-driven, open-source police shooting data, including the *Post* (Ozkan, Worrall & Zettler, 2017).

*what would be defined as unarmed other than print etc.*

*+ 2 reasons : ① Agencies don't report ③ No uniform definition*

Interestingly, the small sample is evidence that unarmed fatalities are very rare events, but it is also a likely source of criticism for external validity. The *Post* database is not complete and is subject to revision;[5] any revisions will alter the results of this study, or any study based on their data. Use of deadly force is a rare event given the volume of contacts officers have with the public (Eith & Durose, 2008), and the small sample limits variability (e.g., sex did not have any variability in the bivariate model and could not be analyzed). The sample size was further reduced when 20 cases were removed because the articles did not disclose enough information to determine whether the officer or the public was facing an imminent threat and so the nature of the encounter was undetermined.[6] Therefore, drawing inferences should be done with some caution.

*reliability*

The data also suffer from limitations described by Jacob (1984); specifically, the news articles are journalistic accounts that may not be reliable. For example, when measuring threats based on the decedent's race (Table 4.6), it is possible that police agencies do not release details of the event consistently based on offender's age, race, or sex. If police agencies release or withhold facts selectively for political purposes, then the media account will be positively or negatively skewed, which leaves the possibility that results of any analysis could change. The news articles also do not capture enough data to analyze the totality of the circumstances, which would provide a much more accurate portrayal of the situation facing the officer at the time force was used. Primary source documents provide unfiltered access to the event, unlike news accounts. For example, it is possible, albeit speculative, that if the entire investigative file was available and data could be extracted from the source documents, then multivariate analysis involving situational variables might yield results similar to Friedrich (1980), who found that "police use of force depends primarily on two types of factors: how the citizen behaves and whether or not other citizens and police are present. . . . The manner of the citizen toward the police has the greatest impact" (p. 95).

It is also possible that some amount of measurement error exists. Accurately measuring constructs that involve a degree of subjectivity in the characteristics of interest—such as categorizing unarmed fatal encounters—may be improved with multiple raters; the coding scheme may have benefitted from inter-rater reliability, but that was not available.

## Policy Implications

Police use of force encounters, both in deadly and non-deadly situations, suffer from a lack of suitable data (Shane, 2016). There is no single data source in the United States from which to make informed decisions about policy and training, or to draw conclusions about the dangerousness of the citizen when the fatality occurred. Pending legislation (H.R. 306, National Statistics on Deadly Force Transparency Act of 2015)[7] would create a comprehensive national government database of incident-level use of force data to support use of force research, policy, and training initiatives. A data source of this type would be consistent with the core mission of the: 1) National Police Research Platform, funded by the National Institute of Justice; 2) National Data Collection Committee of the Division of Policing at the American Society of Criminology; 3) findings from a joint report issued by the National Sheriff's Association and the Treatment Advocacy Center (2013) on justifiable homicides by law enforcement officers involving the mentally ill; 4) findings from the Police Executive Research Forum (2012) on being proactive about preventing use of force situations; 5) Police Foundation's report titled "5 Things You Need to Know About Open Data in Policing;" and 6) President's "Police Data Initiative." A comprehensive data source could inform training practices on use of force transactions from various decision-making stages (Arslan & Farkas, 2015).

## Directions for Future Research

Most previous use of force research tries to explain relationships or the outcome based on sociodemographic factors (e.g., age, race, sex, poverty) in the same way those factors are used to explain crime. Those factors do very little, if anything, to help understand the dynamics of a police shooting, or to help reduce use of force encounters, which should be the overriding goal of use of force research (see Shane, 2016, p. 14 for a proposed use of force research agenda). To better understand how a police shooting unfolds, policing researchers should turn to the factors courts consider when analyzing the legal aspects of a use of force episode, which includes patterns, practices, and the micro interactions between the officer and the citizen in relation to their environment, as set within the prevailing legal framework (*City of Canton v. Harris*, 1989; *Graham v. Connor*, 1989; *Monell v. New York City Department of Social Services*, 1978; *Tennessee v. Garner*, 1985). Most currently available data sources do not enable this type of analysis, which leaves policing virtually unable to learn from previous fatal encounters, particularly unjustified encounters (Henriquez, 1999, p. 21).

Provided reliable incident-level use of force data become available, then path analysis can be used to estimate the magnitude and significance of hypothesized causal connections between sets of variables such as officer, offender, environment, and outcome (i.e., indictment and conviction). As a causal modeling technique, path analysis can examine whether a pattern of inter-correlations among variables fits an underlying theory of which variables are causing the other. Although aspects of a path model are correlational, which has implications for causal inference, if two or more causal hypotheses can be represented in a single path model, then the relative sizes of path coefficients in the model may reveal which of them is better supported by the data. Since causal relationships among variables are examined based on their temporal precedence (Sprinthall, 2007), it would be interesting to develop a model that shows how a police shooting develops, then which of those shootings end in indictment and which of those indictments end in conviction. The path from first encounter to outcome (indictment◊conviction or acquittal) is admittedly very complex and is complicated by the seemingly infinite number of possible causal sequences. A path model is merely a formal specification of the researcher's belief about a how a shooting develops and its eventual outcome, and that belief necessitates variables that may be outside police control (e.g., those that reside with the prosecutor or the jury), which are neither easily measured nor linear.

Previous research demonstrates the contingencies upon which decisions are made and how one decision affects another later in the encounter (Binder & Scharf, 1980). Binder and Scharf (1980) identified five decision stages during a police-citizen encounter: 1) anticipation; 2) entry and initial confrontation; 3) dialogue and information exchange; 4) final frame decision; and 5) aftermath. Cognitive science already demonstrates how threats influence distance perception and how anxiety changes the relationship between distance and perceived threat. Borrowing another concept from cognitive science known as script analysis (Abelson, 1976, 1981; Fayol & Monteil, 1988), the five stages of a police-citizen encounter could examine the decision-making process in greater detail. Script analysis is a useful analytic device for looking at behavioral routines and for generating and organizing knowledge about the procedural aspects, dependencies, and contingencies during a use of force transaction (Davies, 2017; Summerfield, 2017). Future research could engage with the wider literature on stereotyping and racial threat, which has much to say on the issue of police decision-making. It is well established that these and other factors influence the decision-making of police officers just as much as everyone else, so the role these factors play when combined with situational circumstances is critical. Data measuring decisions at each sequential stage of the encounter could be used to develop situational awareness, and with greater awareness comes the ability to preempt (i.e., deescalate) a use of force episode.

Lastly, one issue left uncovered is "American exceptionalism," an ideology grounded in personal liberty and individualism over collectivism. Some context is needed to frame the discussion of police use of fatal force, not least of which is that even if all the shootings presented in this paper are justified or genuine mistakes, 112 unarmed people still lost their lives over a two-year period. This is a figure far higher than comparable advanced democracies (e.g., Australia, Austria, France, Denmark, England and Wales, Finland, Germany, Netherlands, Norway) and what accounts for these differences must be examined to ensure best practices are adopted. One notable aspect of American exceptionalism is the presence of guns, both legal and illegal. Police officers are exposed to wide variation in gun laws across the country (e.g., stand your ground, self-defense, or castle doctrines; open carry; concealed carry; lawful possession of assault weapons; peaceable journey doctrine) that may expose them to more actual or perceived threats, or at least place them in a heightened state of caution during citizen encounters (Hepburn & Hemenway, 2004; Siegel, Ross & King, 2013; Swedler et al., 2015). This is compounded by the geographical diversity of American police departments, most of which are quite small (fewer than 15 officers) suburban and rural agencies, with single officer patrols and disbursed officer back-up. These variations influence policy, training, officer response, and the ability to preempt or avoid a use of force.

## Notes

1  For a complete treatment of the Michael Brown investigation, see Department of Justice Report Regarding The Criminal Investigation Into The Shooting Death Of Michael Brown By Ferguson, Missouri Police Officer Darren Wilson, March 4, 2016, U.S. Department of Justice. Retrieved on July 1, 2017 from www.justice. gov/sites/default/files/opa/press-releases/attachments/2015/03/04/doj_report_ on_shooting_of_michael_brown_1.pdf.
2  The *Post* classifies Brown as unarmed (ID# 1225 of the *Post* data file).
3  See Null et al. (2005) for a meta-analysis of health statistics, which concludes that "American medicine frequently causes more harm than good. . . . It is evident that the American medical system is the leading cause of death and injury in the United States" (p. 1).
4  Following the *Garner* decision in 1985, police departments across the country not only changed their policies to reflect the new national standard, but went beyond the Supreme Court's baseline to limit situations when officers could discharge their firearms such as eliminating warning shots or limiting firing at or from a moving vehicle (see New Jersey Attorney General's policy on use of force as one example: "A law enforcement officer shall not discharge a weapon as a signal for help or as a warning shot" (p. 6); "A law enforcement officer shall not fire a weapon solely to disable moving vehicles" (p. 6) (revised June 2000, Retrieved on July 19, 2017 from www.nj.gov/oag/dcj/agguide/useofforce2001.pdf).
5  The *Post* provides an email address for users to submit an update or correction to an existing case, or submit a new unlisted case (Retrieved on October 24, 2017 from https://washingtonpost.wufoo.com/forms/ help-report-fatal-shootings-by-police-in-the-us/).
6  The cases that were removed only described the encounter in very vague terms or with no details such as "[officers were] involved in a physical altercation," "[the officer] commanded him to stop, but shot him multiple times after he failed to comply," "[the officers] encountered [the man who was] uncooperative and a shooting ensued," and "details of what led deputies to shoot into the house were not immediately available," and "a deputy shot and killed an unarmed man while attempting to serve a narcotics search warrant."
7  Pending as of July 2017. Retrieved on April 1, 2017 from www.congress.gov/ bill/114th-congress/house-bill/306/actions.

# References

Abelson, R. P. (1976). Script processing in attitude formation and decision making. In J. D. Carroll & J. Payne (eds.), *Cognition and Social Behavior*. Hillsdale, NJ: Erlbaum.

Abelson, R. P. (1981). Psychological status of the script concept. *American Psychologist, 36*(7), 715–729.

Alpert, G. P. (2016). Toward a national database of officer-involved shootings. *Criminology & Public Policy, 15*(1), 237–242.

Alpert, G. P., & Dunham, R. G. (1992). *Policing Urban America*. Prospect Heights, IL: Waveland Press.

Alpert, G. P., Dunham, R. G., & MacDonald, J. M. (2004). Interactive police—citizen encounters that result in force. *Police Quarterly, 7*(4), 475–488.

Alpert, G. P., & Smith, W. C. (1994). How reasonable is the reasonable man? Police and excessive force. *The Journal of Criminal Law and Criminology, 85*(2), 481–501.

Amendola, K. L., Weisburd, D., Hamilton, E. E., Jones, G., & Slipka, M. (2011). An experimental study of compressed work schedules in policing: Advantages and disadvantages of various shift lengths. *Journal of Experimental Criminology, 7*(4), 407–442.

American Bar Association. (1980). *Standards on Urban Police Function. Chapter 1, ABA Standards for Criminal Justice: Volume I*, 2nd ed. Retrieved on May 20, 2017 from www.americanbar.org/publications/criminal_justice_section_archive/crim-just_standards_urbanpolice.html

American Heritage Dictionary of the English Language. (1996). *The American Heritage Dictionary of the English Language*, 3rd ed. New York: Houghton Mifflin.

Arnold, T. W. (1962). *The Symbols of Government*, Vol. 13. New York: Harcourt, Brace & World.

Arslan, H., & Farkas, D. (September, 2015). SHOT: Developing a database for police shooting incidents in the United States. In *Internet Technologies and Applications (ITA), 2015* (pp. 85–90). Wrexham, U.K: IEEE.

Austin, A., Proescholdbell, S., & Norwood, T. (2015). 0017 violent deaths among first responders: Using North Carolina violent death reporting system data to inform injury programs. *Injury Prevention, 21*, A6.

Auten, J. H. (1988). Preparing written guidelines. *FBI Law Enforcement Bulletin*, 57(5), 1–7.

Barrett, J., & Belkin, D. (July 10, 2016). Minnesota gov. Mark Dayton says race played a role in fatal police shooting of black man. *The Wall Street Journal*. Retrieved on July 21, 2017 from www.wsj.com/articles/police-fatally-shoot-man-during-traffic-stop-in-minnesota-1467875899

Barrick, K., Hickman, M. J., & Strom, K. J. (2014). Representative policing and violence towards the police. *Policing*, 8(2), 193–204.

Bauerlien, V., & McWhirter, C. (September 23, 2016). Charlotte authorities seek to restore order after two nights of violence. *The Wall Street Journal*. Retrieved on July 21, 2017 from www.wsj.com/articles/charlotte-authorities-seek-to-restore-order-after-night-of-protests-1474556088

Bennell, C., & Jones, N. J. (2005). *The Effectiveness of Use of Force Simulation Training Final Report*. Ottowa: Psychology Department, Carleton University.

Binder, A., & Scharf, P. (1980). The violent police-citizen encounter. *The Annals of the American Academy of Political and Social Science*, 452(1), 111–121.

Blair, J. P., Pollock, J., Montague, D., Nichols, T., Curnutt, J., & Burns, D. (2011). Reasonableness and reaction time. *Police Quarterly*, 14(4), 323–343.

Blanton, H., Jaccard, J., & Burrows, C. N. (2015). Implications of the implicit association test D-transformation for psychological assessment. *Assessment*, 22(4), 429–440.

Bozeman, W. P., Stopyra, J. P., Klinger, D. A., Martin, B. P., Graham, D. D., Johnson III, J. C., Mahoney-Tesoriero, K., & Vail, S. J. (2018). Injuries associated with police use of force. *Journal of Trauma and Acute Care Surgery*, 84(3), 466–472.

Brendl, C. M., Markman, A. B., & Messner, C. (2001). How do indirect measures of evaluation work? Evaluating the inference of prejudice in the implicit association test. *Journal of Personality and Social Psychology*, 81(5), 760.

Buckley, M., Wang, S., Martin, R., & Mack, J. (July 15, 2017). After police shooting of unarmed man, IMPD to change use-of-force policy. *INDYStar.com*.

Bureau of Justice Statistics. (2016). National sources of law enforcement employment data. *U.S. Department of* Justice. Retrieved on December 12, 2017 from www.bjs.gov/content/pub/pdf/nsleed.pdf

Calacal, C. (2017). American is suffering from a plague of deadly, unaccountable and racist police violence. *Salon*. Retrieved on July 16, 2017 from www.salon.com/2017/07/07/america-is-suffering-from-a-plague-of-deadly-unaccountable-and-racist-police-violence_partner/

Cannel, J. M. (2017). *Title 2C: New Jersey Criminal Code Annotated*. Newark, NJ: Gann Law Books.

Chamberlain, S. (March 13, 2017). Martha MacCallum confronts Ferguson documentary filmmaker. *FoxNews*. Retrieved on July 21, 2017 from www.foxnews.com/us/2017/03/13/martha-maccallum-confronts-ferguson-documentary-filmmaker.html

Clarke, R. V., & Eck, J. E. (2005). *Crime Analysis for Problem Solvers*. Washington, DC: Center for Problem Oriented Policing.

Clines, F. X. (March 9, 1993). Police-killers offer insights into victims' fatal mistakes. *New York Times*.

Cole, S., Balcetis, E., & Dunning, D. (2013). Affective signals of threat increase perceived proximity. *Psychological Science*, 24(1), 34–40.

Crifasi, C. K., Pollack, K. M., & Webster, D. W. (2016). Assaults against US law enforcement officers in the line-of-duty: Situational context and predictors of lethality. *Injury Epidemiology, 3*(1), 29.

Davies, A. J. (2017). Shoot/do not shoot—what are the influences? The police recruit perspective. *Policing and Society, 27*(5), 494–507.

Doerner, W. G. (1991). Police unholstering and shooting behavior under simulated field conditions. *American Journal of Police, 10*(3), 1–15.

Eith, C., & Durose, M. R. (2011). *Contacts between police and the public, 2008.* U.S. Washington, DC.: U.S. Department of Justice.

Eitle, D. (2005). The influence of mandatory arrest policies, police organizational characteristics, and situational variables on the probability of arrest in domestic violence cases. *Crime & Delinquency, 51*(4), 573–597.

Erikson, E. H. (1959/1980). *Identity and the Life Cycle.* New York: Norton.

Erikson, E. H. (1963). *Childhood and Society,* 2nd ed. New York: Norton.

Fayol, M., & Monteil, J. M. (1988). The notion of script: From general to developmental and social psychology. *Cahiers de Psychologie Cognitive/European Bulletin of Cognitive Psychology, 8*(4), 335–361.

Federal Bureau of Investigation. (August 3, 2017). *FBI Intelligence Assessment, Black Identity Extremists Likely Motivated to Target Law Enforcement Officers.* Washington, DC: US Department of Justice, Federal Bureau of Investigation. Retrieved on October 10, 2017 from https://assets.documentcloud.org/documents/4067711/BIE-Redacted.pdf

Fiedler, K., Messner, C., & Bluemke, M. (2006). Unresolved problems with the "I", the "A", and the "T": A logical and psychometric critique of the implicit association test (IAT). *European Review of Social Psychology, 17*(1), 74–147.

Fox, J. A., & Levin, J. (2005). *Extreme Killing: Understand Serial and Mass Murder.* Thousand Oaks, CA: Sage.

Freilich, J. D., Chermak, S. M., Belli, R., Gruenewald, J. A., & Parkin, W. S. (2014). Introducing the United States extremist crime database (ECDB). *Terrorism and Political Violence, 26,* 372–384.

Fridell, L. A., & Binder, A. (1992). Police officer decision-making in potentially violent confrontations. *Journal of Criminal Justice, 20*(5), 385–399.

Fridell, L., Faggiani, D., Taylor, B., Brito, C. S., & Kubu, B. (2009). The impact of agency context, policies, and practices on violence against police. *Journal of criminal justice, 37*(6), 542–552.

Friedrich, R. J. (1980). Police use of force: Individuals, situations, and organizations. *The Annals of the American Academy of Political and Social Science, 452*(1), 82–97.

Fyfe, J. J. (1979). Administrative interventions on police shooting discretion: An empirical examination. *Journal of Criminal Justice, 7*(4), 309–323.

Fyfe, J. J. (1988). Police use of deadly force: Research and reform. *Justice Quarterly, 5*(2), 165–205.

Gain, C. (1971). *Discharge of Firearms Policy: Effecting Justice through Administrative Regulation.* Unpublished memorandum, p. 23.

Gillespie, T., Hart, D., & Boren, J. (1998). *Police Use of Force: A Line Officer's Guide.* Shawnee Mission, KS: Varro Press.

Goff, P. A., Eberhardt, J. L., Williams, M. J., & Jackson, M. C. (2008). Not yet human: Implicit knowledge, historical dehumanization, and contemporary consequences. *Journal of Personality and Social Psychology, 94*(2), 292.

Goldstein, H. (1967). Police policy formulation: A proposal for improving police performance. *The Michigan Law Review Association, 65*(6), 1123–1146.

Gruenewald, J. (2012). Are anti-LGBT homicides in the United States unique? *Journal of Interpersonal Violence, 27*(18), 3601–3623.

Gruenewald, J. (2013). Using open-source data to study bias homicide against homeless persons. *International Journal of Criminology and Sociology, 2*, 538–549.

Harding, R. W., & Fahey, R. P. (1973). Killings by Chicago police, 1969–70: An empirical study. *Southern California Law Review, 46*, 284–316.

Henriquez, M. (1999). IACP national database project on police use of force. In National Institute of Justice (ed.), *Use of Force by Police: Overview of National and Local Data*. Washington, DC: National Institute of Justice.

Hepburn, L. M., & Hemenway, D. (2004). Firearm availability and homicide: A review of the literature. *Aggression and Violent Behavior, 9*(4), 417–440.

Hernandez, D., & Repart, P. (November 29, 2016). Olango's father calls for DOJ probe of police shooting. *The San Diego Union-Tribune*. Retrieved on July 21, 2017 from www.sandiegouniontribune.com/news/public-safety/sd-me-olango-doj-20161129-story.html

Hernandez, M. (August 12, 2016). Activists demand state-level prosecutor review police shootings amid Ezell Ford death. *ABC.com*. Retrieved on July 21, 2017 from http://abc7.com/news/activists-demand better-reviews-in-police-shootings-amid-ezell-ford-case/1467309/

Hessl, S. M. (2003). Introduction to the history, demographics, and health effects of law enforcement work. *Clinics in Occupational and Environmental Medicine, 3*(3), 369–384.

Ho, T. (1994). Individual and situational determinants of the use of deadly force: A simulation. *American Journal of Criminal Justice, 18*(1), 41–60.

Hobbes, T. (1651/2012). *Leviathan*. G. A. J. Rogers & K. Schulam (eds.), Part I, Chapter 13. New York: Continuum International Publishing.

Holmes, S. T., Reynolds, K. M., Holmes, R. M., & Faulkner, S. (1998). Individual and situational determinants of police force: An examination of threat presentation. *American Journal of Criminal Justice, 23*(1), 83–106.

International Association of Chiefs of Police. (January, 2017). *National Consensus Policy on Use of Force*. Alexandria, VA: International Association of Chiefs of Police.

Jacob, H. (1984). *Using Published Data: Errors and Remedies*, Vol. 42. Thousand Oaks, CA: Sage.

Jacobs, D., & Britt, D. (1979). Inequality and police use of deadly force: An empirical assessment of a conflict hypothesis. *Social Problems, 26*(4), 403–412.

James, L., Klinger, D., & Vila, B. (2014). Racial and ethnic bias in decisions to shoot seen through a stronger lens: Experimental results from high-fidelity laboratory simulations. *Journal of Experimental Criminology, 10*(3), 323–340.

Jenness, V., & Grattet, R. (2005). The law-in-between: The effects of organizational perviousness on the policing of hate crimes. *Social Problems, 52*(3), 337–359.

Johnson, R. (July, 2016). Dispelling myths surrounding police use of lethal force. *Dolan Consulting Group*. Retrieved on July 19, 2017 from www.dolanconsulting-group.com/wp-content/uploads/2016/07/Dispelling_the_Myths_July18.pdf

Johnson, R. (May, 2017). Examining the facts on implicit bias. *Research Brief*. Dolan Consulting Group. Retrieved on January 20, 2018 from www.dolanconsulting-group.com/wp-content/uploads/2017/05/RB_Implicit-Bias_May-2017-1.pdf

Kaminski, R. J., & Marvell, T. B. (2002). A comparison of changes in police and general homicides: 1930–1998. *Criminology, 40*(1), 171–190.

Kerner Commission. (1968). *National Advisory Commission on Civil Disorder*. Washington, DC: US Government Printing Office.

King, R. D. (2007). The context of minority group threat: Race, institutions, and complying with hate crime law. *Law & Society Review, 41*(1), 189–224.

Kobler, A. L. (1975a). Police homicide in a democracy. *Journal of Social Issues, 31*(1), 163–184.

Kobler, A. L. (1975b). Figures (and perhaps some facts) on police killing of civilians in the United States, 1965–1969. *Journal of Social Issues, 31*(1), 185–191.

Kutzke, L. R. (1980). The department manual: An organizational necessity. *Police Chief, 47*, 46–47.

Kyle, K. (June 29, 2014). Police fail to report deadly shootings. *The Orange County Register (Santa Ana, CA)*. Retrieved on January 20, 2018 from www.ocregister.com/2014/07/02/police-fail-to-report-many-deadly-shootings/

LaFree, G., & Dugan, L. (2007). Introducing the global terrorism database. *Terrorism and Political Violence, 19*(2), 181–204.

Lawton, B. A. (2007). Levels of nonlethal force: An examination of individual, situational, and contextual factors. *Crime & Delinquency, 44*(2), 163–184.

Lewinski, W. J., Seefeldt, D. A., Redmann, C., Gonin, M., Sargent, S., Dysterheft, J. & Thiem, P. (2016). The speed of a prone subject. *Law Enforcement Executive Forum, 16*(1), 70–83.

Little, R. J. A., & Rubin, D. B. (1987). *Statistical Analysis with Missing Data*. New York: John Wiley and Sons.

Loftin, C., Wiersema, B., McDowall, D., & Dobrin, A. (2003). Underreporting of justifiable homicides committed by police officers in the United States, 1976–1998. *American Journal of Public Health, 93*(7), 1117–1121.

Lyons, K., Radburn, C., Orr, R., & Pope, R. (2017). A profile of injuries sustained by law enforcement officers: A critical review. *International Journal of Environmental Research and Public Health, 14*(2), 142.

MacDonald, H. (February 8, 2016). Black and unarmed: Behind the numbers. *The Marshall Project*. Retrieved on February 22, 2017 from www.themarshallproject.org/2016/02/08/black-and-unarmed-behind-the-numbers#.sAig0zaTu

Mastrofski, S. D., & Ritti, R. R. (1992). You can lead a horse to water. . .: A case study of a police department's response to stricter drunk-driving laws. *Justice Quarterly, 9*(3), 465–491.

Mastrofski, S. D., Ritti, R. R., & Hoffmaster, D. (1987). Organizational determinants of police discretion: The case of drinking and driving. *Journal of Criminal Justice, 15*(5), 387–402.

Mastrofski, S. D., Ritti, R. R., & Snipes, J. B. (1994). Expectancy theory and police productivity in DUI enforcement. *Law & Society Review*, *28*(1), 113–148.

McCluskey, J. D., Terrill, W., & Paoline, III, E. A. (2005). Peer group aggressiveness and the use of coercion in police—suspect encounters. *Police Practice and Research*, *6*(1), 19–37.

McEwen, T. (1996). *National Data Collection on Police Use of Force*. Washington, DC: Bureau of Justice Statistics and National Institute of Justice.

Meyer, M. W. (1980). Police shootings at minorities: The case of Los Angeles. *The Annals of the American Academy of Political and Social Science*, *452*(1), 98–110.

Miller, T. R., Lawrence, B. A., Carlson, N. N., Hendrie, D., Randall, S., Rockett, I. R., & Spicer, R. S. (2017). Perils of police action: A cautionary tale from US data sets. *Injury Prevention*, *23*(1), 27–32.

Milton, C. H., Halleck, J. W., Lardner, L., & Abrecht, G. L. (1977). *Police Use of Deadly Force*. Washington, DC: Police Foundation.

Morabito, M. S., & Socia, K. M. (2015). Is dangerousness a myth? Injuries and police encounters with people with mental illnesses. *Criminology & Public Policy*, *14*(2), 253–276.

National Institute of Justice. (1999). *Use of Force by Police: Overview of National and Local Data*, NCJ# 176330. Washington, DC: National Institute Justice.

Neyfakh, L. (December 28, 2015). Tamir Rice's death resulted from "Officer-Created Jeopardy." So why were no officers indicted. *The Slatest*. Retrieved on February 17, 2017 from www.slate.com/blogs/the_slatest/2015/12/28/tamir_rice s death didn_t_lead_to_indictments_because_of_supreme_court_vagueness.html?wpsrc=sh_all_mob_em_ru

Nieuwenhuys, A., Cañal-Bruland, R., & Oudejans, R. D. (2012). Effects of threat on police officers' shooting behavior: Anxiety, action specificity, and affective influences on perception. *Applied Cognitive Psychology*, *26*(4), 608–615.

Nix, J., Campbell, B. A., Byers, E. H., & Alpert, G. P. (2017). A bird's eye view of civilians killed by police in 2015: Further evidence of implicit bias. *Criminology & Public Policy*, *16*(1), 1–32.

Noble, J.J. & Alpert, G.P. (2015). State-created Danger: Should Officer Be Accountable for Reckless Tactical Decision Making? In, Roger G. Dunham and Geoffrey P. Alpert (eds). *Critical issues in policing: Contemporary readings*. (pp. 567–582). Waveland Press.

Norusis, M. J. (2010). *PASW Statistics 18 Guide to Data Analysis*. Upper Saddle River, NJ: Prentice Hall Press.

Null, G., Dean, C., Feldman, M., Rasio, D., & Smith, D. (2005). Death by medicine. *Journal of Orthomolecular Medicine*, *20*(1), 21–34.

O'Loughlin, M. G. (1990). What is bureaucratic accountability and how can we measure it? *Administration & Society*, *22*(3), 275–302.

Oswald, F., Mitchell, G., Blanton, H., Jaccard, J., & Tetlock, P. (2013). Predicting ethnic and racial discrimination: A meta-analysis of IAT criterion studies. *Journal of Personality and Social Psychology*, *105*(2), 171–192.

Oswald, F., Mitchell, G., Blanton, H., Jaccard, J., & Tetlock, P. (2015). Using the IAT to predict ethnic and racial discrimination: Small effect sizes of unknown societal significance. *Journal of Personality and Social Psychology Studies*, *108*(4), 562–571.

Owusu-Bempah, A. (2016). Race and policing in historical context: Dehumaniza-tion and the policing of Black people in the 21st century. *Theoretical Criminology* (online ahead of print).

Ozkan, T., Worrall, J. L., & Zettler, H. (2017). Validating media-driven and crowd-sourced police shooting data: A research note. *Journal of Crime and Justice, 1–12.*

Paoline, E. A., & Terrill, W. (2005). Women police officers and the use of coercion. *Women & Criminal Justice, 15*(3–4), 97–119.

Parkin, W. S., & Gruenewald, J. (2017). Open-source data and the study of homicide. *Journal of Interpersonal Violence, 32*(18), 2693–2723.

Petersson, U., Bertilsson, J., Fredriksson, P., Magnusson, M., & Fransson, P. A. (2017). Police officer involved shootings—retrospective study of situational char-acteristics. *Police Practice and Research, 18*(3), 306–321.

Petrowski, T. D. (2002). Use of force polices and training. *FBI Law Enforcement Bulletin, 71*(10), 25–32.

Phillips, T., & Smith, P. (2000). Police violence occasioning citizen complaint. *British Journal of Criminology, 40*(3), 480–496.

Pichon, S., de Gelder, B., & Grezes, J. (2012). Threat prompts defensive brain responses independently of attentional control. *Cerebral Cortex, 22*(2), 274–285.

Pickett, J. T., Mancini, C., Mears, D. P., & Gertz, M. (2015). Public (mis)understand-ing of crime policy: The effects of criminal justice experience and media reliance. *Criminal Justice Policy Review, 26*(5), 500–522.

Pinizzotto, A. J., Davis, E. F., Bohrer, S. B., & Infanti, B. J. (2012). Law enforcement restraint in the use of deadly force within the context of "the deadly mix". *Interna-tional Journal of Police Science & Management, 14*(4), 285–298.Pinizzotto, A. J., Davis, E. F., & Miller, C. (2000). Officers' perceptual shorthand: What messages are citizens sending to law enforcement officers? *FBI Law Enforcement Bulletin, 69*(7), 1–6.

Pinizzotto, A. J., Davis, E. F., & Miller, C. (2006). *Violent Encounters: A Study of Felonious Assaults on Our Nation's Law Enforcement Officers.* Washington, DC: U.S. Department of Justice, Federal Bureau of Investigation, National Institute of Justice.

Quinet, K. (2011). Prostitutes as victims of serial homicide: Trends and case charac-teristics, 1970–2009. *Homicide Studies, 15*(1), 74–100.

Reiss, A. J. Jr. (1968). Police brutality—answers to key questions. *Trans-action, 5,* 10–19.

Reiss, A. J. Jr. (1980). Controlling police use of deadly force. *The Annals of the American Academy of Political and Social Science, 452*(1), 122–134.

Ridgeway, G. (2016). Officer risk factors associated with police shootings: A matched case—control study. *Statistics and Public Policy, 3*(1), 1–6. Retrieved on January 20, 2018 from www.tandfonline.com/doi/pdf/10.1080/2330443X.2015.11 29918?needAccess=true

Robin, G. D. (1963). Justifiable homicide by police officers. *The Journal of Criminal Law, Criminology & Police Science, 54*(2), 225–231.

Rousseau, J. J. (1968). *The Social Contract,* Maurice Cranston (trans.). England: Pen-guin Books. (Original work published 1762).

Schultz, M., & Withrow, B. L. (2004). Racial profiling and organizational change. *Criminal Justice Policy Review, 15*(4), 462–485.

Shane, J. M. (2016). Improving police use of force: A policy essay on national data collection. *Criminal Justice Policy Review*, 1–21 (online ahead of print).

Shane, J. M., Lawton, B., & Swenson, Z. (2017). The prevalence of fatal police shootings by U.S. police, 2015–2016: Patterns and answers from a new data set. *Journal of Criminal Justice, 52*, 101–111.

Sherman, L. W. (1980). Execution without trial: Police homicide and the constitution. *Vanderbilt Law Review, 33*, 71–100.

Sherman, L. W., & Berk, R. A. (1984). The specific deterrent effects of arrest for domestic assault. *American Sociological Review, 49*(2), 261–272.

Sherman, L. W., Cohn, E. G., & Gartin, P. R. (1986). *Citizens Killed by Big City Police, 1970–84.* Washington, DC: Crime Control Institute.

Sherman, L. W., & Langworthy, R. H. (1979). Measuring homicide by police officers. *Journal of Criminal Law & Criminology, 70*(4), 546–560.

Sidanius, J., Van Laar, C., Levin, S., & Sinclair, S. (2003). Social hierarchy maintenance and assortment into social roles: A social dominance perspective. *Group Processes & Intergroup Relations, 6*(4), 333–352.

Siegel, M., Ross, C. S., & King III, C. (2013). The relationship between gun ownership and firearm homicide rates in the United States, 1981–2010. *American Journal of Public Health, 103*(11), 2098–2105.

Singal, J. (January 11, 2017), Psychology's favorite tool for measuring racism isn't up to the job. *New York Magazine.* Retrieved on January 22, 2017 from http://nymag.com/scienceofus/2017/01/psychologys-racism-measuring-tool-isnt-up-to-the-job.html

Smith, B. L., & Damphousse, K. R. (2007). *American Terrorism Study, 1980–2002* (ICPSR04639-v1). Ann Arbor, MI: Inter-university Consortium for Political and Social Research [distributor]. doi:10.3886/ICPSR04639.v1

Smith, R. J., Levinson, J. D., & Robinson, Z. (2014). Implicit white favoritism in the criminal justice system. *Alabama Law Review, 66*(4), 871–923.

Sprinthall, R. C. (2007). *Basic Statistical Analysis*, 8th ed. Boston, MA: Allyn & Bacon.

Stamps, A. I. (2012). How distance mitigates perceived threat at 30–90 m. *Perceptual and Motor Skills, 114*(3), 709–716.

Sullivan, S. P., & Gallo, B. Jr. (February 10, 2017). N.J. trooper cleared over "wrong house" shooting of 76-year old man. *NJ.com.* Retrieved on June 10, 2017 from www.nj.com/news/index.ssf/2017/02/nj_trooper_cleared_over_wrong_house_shooting_of_76.html

Summerfield, T. S. L. (2017). *Police Decision-Making: The Impact of Choice on Use-of-Force Decisions* (Doctoral dissertation, Faculty of Graduate Studies and Research, University of Regina).

Swedler, D. I., Simmons, M. M., Dominici, F., & Hemenway, D. (2015). Firearm prevalence and homicides of law enforcement officers in the United States. *American Journal of Public Health, 105*(10), 2042–2048.

Sykes, R. E., & Clark, J. P. (1975). A theory of deference exchange in police-civilian encounters. *American Journal of Sociology, 81*(3), 584–600.

Tennenbaum, A. N. (1994). The influence of the Garner decision on police use of deadly force. *Journal of Criminal Law and Criminology, 85*(1), 241–260.

Terrill, W. (2009). The elusive nature of reasonableness. *Criminology & Public Policy, 8*(1), 163–172.

Terrill, W., & Paoline III, E. A. (2017). Police use of less lethal force: Does administrative policy matter? *Justice Quarterly, 34*(2), 193–216.

Tiesman, H. M., Hendricks, S. A., Bell, J. L., & Amandus, H. A. (2010). Eleven years of occupational mortality in law enforcement: The census of fatal occupational injuries, 1992–2002. *American Journal of Industrial Medicine, 53*(9), 940–949.

Tiesman, H. M., William, M. G., Konda, S., Rojek, J., & Marsh, S. (2018). Nonfatal injuries to law enforcement officers: A rise in assaults. *American Journal of Preventive Medicine, 54*(4), 503–509.

U.S. Department of Justice. (March 4, 2015). *Department of Justice Report Regarding the Criminal Investigation Into the Shooting Death of Michael Brown by Ferguson, Missouri Police Officer Darren Wilson.* Washington, DC: U.S. Department of Justice. Retrieved on June 20, 2017 from www.justice.gov/sites/default/files/opa/press-releases/attachments/2015/03/04/doj_report_on_shooting_of_michael_brown_1.pdf

Walker, S. (2010). *The New World of Police Accountability.* Thousand Oaks, CA: Sage.

Weisburd, D., Petrosino, A., & Mason, G. (1993). Design sensitivity in criminal justice experiments. *Crime and Justice, 17,* 337–379.

Welsh, W. N., & Harris, P. W. (2004). *Criminal Justice Policy and Planning,* 2nd ed. Cincinnati, OH: Anderson.

Wheeler, A., Phillips, S. W., Worrall, J. L., & Bishopp, S. A. (in press). What factors influence an officer's decision to shoot? The promise and limitations of using public data. *Journal of Research and Policy.* First Published Online March 26, 2018.

Whitbourne, S. K., Zuschlag, M. K., Elliot, L. B., & Waterman, A. S. (1992). Psychosocial development in adulthood: A 22-year sequential study. *Journal of Personality and Social Psychology, 63*(2), 260–271.

White, M. D. (2001). Controlling police decisions to use deadly force: Reexamining the importance of administrative policy. *Crime & Delinquency, 47*(1), 131–151.

Wiersema, B., Loftin, C., & McDowall, D. (2000). A comparison of supplementary homicide reports and national vital statistics system homicide estimates for US counties. *Homicide Studies, 4*(4), 317–340.

Williams, H. E., Bowman, S. W., & Jung, J. T. (2016). The limitations of government databases for analyzing fatal officer-involved shootings in the United States. *Criminal Justice Policy Review.* doi:10.1177/0887403416650927

Worden, R. E. (1989). Situational and attitudinal explanations of police behavior: A theoretical reappraisal and empirical assessment. *Law and Society Review, 23,* 667–711.

Worrall, J. L., Bishopp, S. A., Zinser, S. C., Wheeler, A. P., & Phillips, S. W. (in press). Exploring bias in police shooting decisions with real shoot/don't shoot cases. *Crime & Delinquency.* First Published Online March 8, 2018.

Yan, H., Shah, K., & Grimberg, E. (May 2, 2017). Ex-officer Michael Slager pleads guilty in shooting death of Walter Scott. *CNN.com.*

## Cases Cited

*Bell v. Wolfish*, 441 U. S. 520, 441 U. S. 559 (1979)

*Brown v. United States*, 256 U.S. 335 (1921)

*City of Canton, Ohio v. Harris* 489 U.S. 378 (1989)

*Deluna v. City of Rockford*, 447 F.3d 1008, 1010 (7th Cir. 2006)

*Florida v. Rodriguez*, 469 U. S. 1, 6 (1984)

*Forrester v. City of San Diego*, 25 F.3d 804, 807–08 (9th Cir.1994)

*Graham v. Connor*, 490 U.S. 386 (1989)

*Hunt v. County of Whitman*, 2006 WL 2096068 (E.D. Wash. 2006)

*Illinois v. Wardlow*, 528 U.S. 119 (2000)

*Krueger v. Fuhr*, 991 F.2d 435 (8th Cir.), cert. denied, 510 U.S. 946 (1993)

*Illinois v. Gates* 462 U.S. 213 (1983)

*Loch v. City of Litchfield*, 689 F.3d 961, 965 (8th Cir. 2012)

*Monell v. Department of Social Services* 436 U.S. 658 (1978)

*Nelson v. County of Wright*, 162 F.3d 986, 990 (8th Cir. 1998)

*O'Bert v. Vargo*, 331 F.3d 29, 36 (2d Cir. 2003)

*Payne v. Pauley*, 337 F.3d 767 (7th Cir. 2003)

*Scott v. Edinburg*, 346 F.3d 752, 756 (7th Cir. 2003)

*Scott v. United States*, 436 U.S. 128, 137-139 (1978)

*Screws v. United States*, 325 U.S. 91 (1945)

*Sharrar v. Felsing*, 128 F.3d 810 (3rd Cir. 1997)

*Tennessee v. Garner* 471 U.S. 1 (1985)

*United States v. Brignoni-Ponce*, 422 U. S. 873, 885 (1975)

*United States v. Dykes*, 406 F.3d 717 (D.C. Cir. 2005)

*United States v. Koon*, 833 F.Supp. 769 (C.D. Cal. 1993), *aff'd in part*, 518 U.S. 81 (1996)

*United States v. Lanier*, 520 U.S. 259 (1997)

*United States v. McClean*, 528 F.2d 1250, 1255 (2d Cir. 1976)

*United States v. Place*, 462 U. S. 696, 462 U. S. 703 (1983)

*United States v. Robinson*, 414 U.S. 218 (1973)

# Index

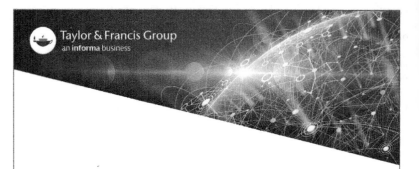

Taylor & Francis Group
an **informa** business

# Taylor & Francis eBooks

www.taylorfrancis.com

A single destination for eBooks from Taylor & Francis
with increased functionality and an improved user
experience to meet the needs of our customers.

90,000+ eBooks of award-winning academic content in
Humanities, Social Science, Science, Technology, Engineering,
and Medical written by a global network of editors and authors.

## TAYLOR & FRANCIS EBOOKS OFFERS:

A streamlined
experience for
our library
customers

A single point
of discovery
for all of our
eBook content

Improved
search and
discovery of
content at both
book and
chapter level

## REQUEST A FREE TRIAL
support@taylorfrancis.com

 Routledge
Taylor & Francis Group

 CRC Press
Taylor & Francis Group